ELOQUENT RAGE

ELOQUENT RAGE

A BLACK FEMINIST DISCOVERS HER SUPERPOWER

BRITTNEY COOPER

ST. MARTIN'S PRESS ≈ NEW YORK

In some instances, names have been changed to protect the individual's right to privacy.

www.stmartins.com

Designed by Anna Gorovoy

Library of Congress Cataloging-in-Publication Data

Names: Cooper, Brittney C., 1980- author.
Title: Eloquent rage : a black feminist discovers her superpower / Brittney Cooper.
Description: First edition. | New York : St. Martin's Press, 2018.
Identifiers: LCCN 2017036275| ISBN 9781250112576 (hardcover) | ISBN 9781250112897 (ebook)
Subjects: LCSH: Cooper, Brittney C., 1980– | African American feminists—Biography. | Feminism—United States.
Classification: LCC HQ1413.C67 C67 2018 | DDC 305.48/8960730092 [B] —dc23
LC record available at https://lccn.loc.gov/2017036275

Our books may be purchased in bulk for promotional, educational, or business use. Please contact your local bookseller or the Macmillan Corporate and Premium Sales Department at 1-800-221-7945, extension 5442, or by email at MacmillanSpecialMarkets@macmillan.com.

First Edition: February 2018

10 9 8 7 6 5 4 3 2 1

FOR GRANDMAMA AND HER DAUGHTERS

CONTENTS

THE PROBLEM
WITH SASS

This is a book by a grown-ass woman written for other grown-ass women. This is a book for women who expect to be taken seriously and for men who take grown women seriously. This is a book for women who know shit is fucked up. These women want to change things but don't know where to begin.

To be clear, I'm not really into self-help books, so I don't have one of those catchy three-step plans for changing the world. What I have is anger. Rage, actually. And that's the place where more women should begin—with the things that make us angry.

When it comes to Black women, sometimes Americans don't recognize that sass is simply a more palatable form of rage. Americans adore sassy Black women. You know, those caricatures of finger-waving, eye-rolling Black women at whom everyone loves to laugh—women like Tyler Perry's Madea, Mammy in *Gone with the Wind*, or Nell from that old eighties sitcom *Gimme a Break!* These kinds of Black women put white folks at ease.

In my first terrible job after college, my boss, an older white woman, told me that the students at the predominantly Black school at which we worked had deemed her an honorary Black woman. When I looked at her with question marks in my eyes, she said, "You know, they mean the way I talk to them and roll my neck," and demonstrated it for me. I went on back to my desk.

Years after that, I was doing a summer abroad in South Korea. My Malaysian roommate, who had seen many episodes of the old nineties sitcom *Family Matters*, told me that she loved Black women because we were sassy like Harriette and Laura Winslow, the main Black female characters on that show. To her, these stereotypical portrayals made Black folks seem understandable, even though to me, her descriptions felt like we were exotic others. She loved it, she said, when Black women put their hands on their hips and swiveled their necks in protest. Not wanting to offend this woman who I otherwise really liked, I simply said, "We're not all like that." She looked disappointed.

I am fat, Black, and Southern. But this is not a sassy Black girl's tale. Black women turn to sass when rage is too risky— because we have jobs to keep, families to feed, and bills to pay. Black women who hold their communities together also hold our broader American community together. But it's unclear whether we are really being taken seriously.

Owning anger is a dangerous thing if you're a fat Black girl like me. Angry Black Women get dismissed all the time. We are told we are irrational, crazy, out of touch, entitled, disruptive, and not team players. The story goes that Angry Black Women scare babies, old people, and grown men. This is absurd. And it is a lie. If you have the nerve to be fat *and* angry, then you are treated as a bully even if you are doing nothing aggressive at all. The truth is that Angry Black Women are looked upon as entities to be contained, as inconvenient citizens who keep on talking about their rights while refusing to do their duty and smile at everyone. Don't you just hate when folks yell at you to "Smile!"? I told the last man who said that shit to me, "*You* smile!"

Some years ago, I ran into a former student on the college campus where I was teaching. Erica was a brilliant Black girl who wrote great papers and asked really smart questions. As we were standing around with a group of others, chatting, she said, "I loved having you as my professor. Your lectures were filled with rage. But it was, like, the most eloquent rage ever." I immediately felt defensive. What did she mean by *rage*? "I'm not angry," I told her. "I'm passionate." By then, I was wary of the Angry Black Woman stereotype. Even though I was only in my mid-twenties at the time, I had already experienced many years of white people doing that thing they do to articulate Black women—always asking us "Why are you so angry?" I hated the accusation from others, usually white people, because it was unfair, a way to discredit the legitimacy of the things Black women say by calling them emotional and irrational. But Erica was a Black girl. She fixed me with a telltale look that only another Black woman can give you, a look that said, *Girl, be for real.* And then she said, "Brittney, you know you're angry." I felt exposed. I couldn't even say anything. She had seen through the veneer, seen the lie I was telling. It was devastating. And life-changing.

I *was* angry. As hell. And I was fooling no one.

Black women have the right to be mad as hell. We have been dreaming of freedom and carving out spaces for liberation since we arrived on these shores. There is no other group, save Indigenous women, that knows and understands more fully the soul of the American body politic than Black women, whose reproductive and social labor have made the world what it is. This is not mere propaganda. Black women know what it means to love ourselves in a world that hates us. We know what it means to do a whole lot with very little, to "make a dollar out of fifteen cents," as it were. We know what it means to snatch dignity from the jaws of power and come out standing. We know what it means to face horrific violence and trauma from both our communities and our nation-state and carry on anyway. But we also scream, and cry, and hurt, and mourn, and struggle. We get heartbroken, our feelings get stepped on, our dreams get crushed. We get angry, and we express that anger. We know what it means to feel invisible.

I know what it means to feel invisible. To be picked on, bullied, misunderstood, and dismissed. But when Erica called me out on my anger, it was clear that she saw me in a way that I wasn't particularly interested in being seen. She helped me to realize that my anger could be a powerful force for good. She had called my rage *eloquent*. Clear. Expressive. To the point. In her estimation, it had made me a good teacher, and it had inspired her and other students.

Over and over again, Black girls have called me out and demanded that I get my shit together, around my rage, around my work in the world, and around my feminism. Those Black girl callouts, or "homegirl interventions," as I call them in this book, have come from my grandmama, my mama, and my girls. And they have saved my life.

America needs a homegirl intervention in the worst way. So in this book, I am doing what Black women do best. I'm calling America out on her bullshit about racism, sexism, classism, homophobia, and a bunch of other stuff.

And I'm using feminism to stage this homegirl intervention. I'm here for picket signs, pussy hats (as long as there are plenty of brown ones in the mix), and patchouli. My picket signs are as likely to say FUCK THE POLICE as they are to say FUCK THE PATRIARCHY. Black-girl feminism is all the rage, and we need all the rage. Feminism can give us a common language for thinking about how sexism, and racism, and classism work together to fuck shit up for everybody.

Like many other feminists, I used to carry around Audre Lorde's book *Sister Outsider* like it was the feminist bible. Her essay "The Uses of Anger: Women Responding to Racism" taught me that rage is a legitimate political emotion. She writes, "Focused with precision, it can become a powerful source of energy serving progress and change."

Here's the thing: My anger and rage haven't always been "focused with precision." The process, of both becoming a feminist and becoming okay with rage as a potential feminist superpower, has been messy as hell. We need to embrace our messiness more. We need to embrace the ways we are in process more. Very often Black girls don't get the opportunity to be in process. So just know that you don't have to have everything figured out to read and enjoy this book.

For more than a decade, since Erica named for me my superpower—eloquent rage—I've been trying to figure out how to focus it with precision.

When I watch the Williams sisters—Venus and Serena—use their power on a tennis court, I feel like they are a case study in how to use rage with precision. Born six months after Venus and nine months before Serena, I feel like I grew up with the Williams sisters. When they first began to win major tournaments in the late 1990s, sportscasters derisively referred to the "power tennis" they played. These strong, athletic Black girls had serves with speeds of more than 120 miles per hour and they scared the shit out of white girls. Until they learned how to use their power, it often became a liability, causing them to make lots of mistakes on and off the court.

But in the nearly twenty years since they have come to dominate tennis, both sisters have figured out how to corral all that power into precise serves and shots that are nearly unmatched. They have created this kind of alchemy that uses their physical strength and strategic prowess on the court, together with all the racial slurs and insults they have endured over the years—being called the N-word, being called ugly, being told their bodies were too manly—to create something that looks magical to the rest of us. Watching Venus play, particularly on grass courts, is like watching a Black girl perform in a ballet. She is an elegant player.

Watching Serena play, particularly when she's beating white women, is like watching eloquent rage personified. Her shots are clear and expressive. Her wins are exultant. Her victories belong to all of us, even though she's the one who does all the work.

That's kind of how it feels to be a Black woman. Like our victories belong to everyone, even though we do all the work. But here's the thing—if I can master any force in my life and slay it like Serena slays tennis balls on the court, then I'm happy to share the wealth.

CAPITAL B,
CAPITAL F

It took nothing short of a homegirl intervention to turn me into a feminist. It was my senior year at Howard University, and I'd managed to go through much of college without having even one boyfriend on campus. As much as Howard offered an explicit education in the workings of racism and white supremacy, its lessons about sexism were far more subtle. I felt like something was wrong with me. The boys wanted me to run their student government campaigns, or they wanted to verbally joust with me, but they didn't want to date me. On high self-esteem days, I simply thought it was because they were dumb. On bad self-esteem days, I thought it was because I was fat. (Fat is of course relative, because if I could be my college size again . . .) I hadn't considered that sexism had anything to do with it, that young men had been socialized to desexualize outspoken women. I reveled in being unconquerable, because that's an important trait for Black girls surviving abusive father figures to have.

I didn't realize that living life in a patriarchy, even in a beautiful Black one, meant that I had to at least *appear* conquerable if I wanted to get chose.

One day, on campus, I proclaimed with the confidence of a twenty-year-old who knows just enough to be dangerous, that "feminism is white women's shit. At most, I'm a womanist." I had heard someone else invoking Alice Walker's definition of womanism, and it sounded good enough to me. The thing is: my defection from feminism wasn't a principled defection. I hadn't read Walker's definition at all. But I had spent a lifetime having slightly awkward friendships with the white girls with whom I grew up, and I had escaped after high school to the Blackness of Howard to recover from all of it. I'll talk more about my complicated relationship with white women in the next chapter, but suffice it to say that I was ready to lay the entirety of my feminist inheritance—the work of women like Sojourner Truth, Anna Julia Cooper, Ida B. Wells, and the women of the Combahee River Collective—on the altar next to all the blond hair that I had mentally burned in effigy after high school. This is what I like to call doing the most, but achieving the least. And, luckily, one of my homegirls saw through my bullshit and staged a friendly but serious intervention.

My friend Tracey heard me making such ignorant pronouncements about feminism and hemmed me up in the dorms later. "Here," she said, handing me a book. "Read this, because you were talking kinda crazy earlier about feminism." This wasn't our first discussion about the f-word. She had also asked me a few months earlier if I wanted to "come to Blackburn [the student center] to hear bell hooks?" "Who is bell hooks?" I had asked, vaguely remembering that I had encountered her name in a book on gender and equality that I had bought during my days on my high school's debate team. "Oh, she writes all this feminist stuff, but she talks real crazy, so it should be interesting," Tracey had said, chuckling.

"Talking crazy" in our college parlance could be either an indictment or a compliment. It was a way to denote those moments of flirtation with ideas that skirted the line between being profound and being absolutely nonsensical. For instance, there was the day that the Honors Office Crew (the Blerds of my day) entertained the idea of whether women might evolve into being able to impregnate themselves, if it happened to be true that clitorises were really just small penises. My good Christian self was both scandalized by the mention of clitorises and penises (and evolution!) but also deeply curious and seduced by the questions themselves. I vacillated between wondering whether my friends were going to hell, and tiptoeing into the deep with them because I secretly loved the irreverence of it all. It felt like any day in the Howard Honors office could lead to a personal evolution of big-bang proportions.

Listening to years of "talking crazy" among the crew had made me fall in love with ideas in a substantive way. For instance, the Crew put me on to Ta-Nehisi Coates back in the early 2000s when he wrote for the *Washington City Paper*. His pieces were must-reads, and when we saw him hanging out on campus, we whispered to each other, stanning ever so slightly. Once, I remember Coates popping his head into a room of Howard student leaders in the Blackburn Center and scowling at us, unimpressed. We were probably having a heated debate about the fate of Black America, and apparently, we weren't saying anything earth shattering. I'm pretty sure I scowled back.

Still, it was cool as hell to run into thinkers on campus whose work I'd read on the regular. I became a Ph.D. because I wanted that kind of life, one where "talking crazy"—playing with ideas that skirted the line between the radical and the absurd, the sacred and the profane—was the order of the day. So I knew that in Tracey's indictment of hooks's propensity to "talk crazy" there was also an endorsement, a belief that she was worth hearing. Curious about just exactly what kind of crazy talk hooks might engage in, I followed Tracey to the panel.

I don't remember much about hooks's talk. Perhaps we had arrived late. I do remember that she seemed unimpressed and perhaps agitated, most likely with the conservative gender politics that shaped Howard during my time there. But hooks's feminist "crazy talk" was my first experience with the kinds of provocations that can be life-changing. And it was quite different from the dismissive "crazy talk" that had me in the hot seat with my homegirl.

I think Tracey had just assumed, naturally, that I would be a feminist, given my fierce sense of selfhood and my willingness to drag anyone who stepped to me with what I deemed a bad argument. She therefore looked at me both curiously and incredulously when I dared to insist otherwise. I took the book, a collection of academic essays on feminist theory. She instructed, "I think you'll really like this essay on multiple jeopardies by Deborah King." Sufficiently chastised, I agreed to read the piece she had chosen. While I was not especially interested in being a feminist, I was even less interested in having a raggedy analysis, of being critically *uninformed*, and of getting caught out there, assed out and looking ignorant. So I sat down that same night, turned to the essay Tracey had suggested, and tried to get clearer on what exactly feminism was and how it might apply to me. King wanted us to see the effects of oppressions on Black women's lives as what she called "multiplicative." Our class position, sexual identity, and many other vectors of power shaped our identity in the world, and more specifically, these things determined how many boots there were on our collective necks.

That essay didn't turn me into a feminist, because it felt a bit too academic for me to read without the benefit of a classroom context to work out the ideas. But I did begin to care deeply about Black women's legacy of activism and ask more questions about what historical Black women had said about issues of racism and sexism. Over the next few years, I would have the opportunity, via some dope-ass Black feminist professors and because of the work of Hip Hop feminist Joan Morgan, to name and own a feminism for myself. But what mattered to me most, what lingers for me now, was the thoughtfulness and care of another Black girl's friendship.

Friendships with Black girls have always saved my life. I give the side eye to any Black woman who doesn't have other Black women friends, to any woman who is prone to talk about how she relates better to men than to women, to anyone who goes on and on about how she "doesn't trust females." If you say fuck the patriarchy but you don't ride for other women, then it might be more true that the patriarchy has fucked you, seducing you with the belief that men care more about your well-being than women do.

It isn't true.

I came up in an era when Black girls loudly proclaimed that *they didn't have friends. They had associates.* It has always rung false to me, maybe because the introverted parts of me had absolutely no interest in spending sustained time fake-grinning at people with whom I couldn't be my whole self. I wanted friends to snicker, giggle, and pass notes with, to share secrets with. I wanted people who would have my back. I worry about a world in which Black girls on their way to becoming women are taught to distrust women. I worry about a world in which Black women who are raising boys cultivate distrust for girls by looking upon every girl who shows interest in their sons with distrust. We wonder why young men hate women and, sometimes, the sad truth is that their mamas and aunts and sisters act as an arm of the patriarchy by parroting the refrain that "girls simply can't be trusted."

It's hard for Black girls to be friends with each other. But there is wonder-working power in the homegirl hem-up, the particular way that Black women friends gather you and save your life by telling you lovingly to get your shit together. It took me a really long time to find my tribe, though. I always knew I needed Black girls to make it, and I longed for their friendship in substantial ways throughout childhood. But, more often than not, I was rebuffed. We live in a world that tells women to distrust other women. And those of us who do dare to love other women hard are taught to distrust our impulses, to see that love as queer and wrong.

I have had more than a few crushes on my homegirls, mostly intellectual and always deeply emotional, and sometimes perhaps a bit sexual. In middle school, when I finally found my first real-deal, pass-notes-in-class, rush-home-after-school-to-talk-on-the-phone-for-several-more-hours Black-girl bestie, I was elated. And a bit surprised. Neisha had sidled up to me one day at the end of seventh grade, as we were walking out the doors toward the buses after school, and said, "We're gonna have to stick together next year." Up until that point, I didn't totally know how I felt about her. She was both smart and cool; I had smart on lock, but couldn't find my own cool even if someone had handed it to me in a paper bag.

Neisha and I had come to know each other better a few weeks earlier on our seventh-grade honors trip to South Louisiana, a place that seemed a world away from our more rural, North Louisiana experience. On the trip, we bonded over an episode of *Martin*, featuring his next-door neighbor Sheneneh and her homegirls Bonquisha and Keylolo. Together with Reina, a Black girl whom I had known since I was eight, when we ended up in Girl Scouts together, the three of us—the only Black girls on the trip—stuck together. For some reason, perhaps because of the insecurities that plague all girls at age twelve, occasionally Neisha and Reina would devolve into mean-girl behaviors with me as the target. Just happy to have Black girls for friends, I pretended not to hear the commentary they made behind my back, about how corny I was, or how naïve I was. One day, in eighth grade, after Neisha and I became actual besties, I heard her walking behind me in the hall, whispering to someone about why I had worn hot-pink scrunch socks instead of white tights with the cute skirt I rocked to school that day. My feelings were hurt; I pretended like I simply didn't hear her. A confrontation would surely have ended our friendship.

One of the final outings of the Louisiana Heritage Tour in 1993 was a trip to New Orleans' Audubon Zoo, the biggest zoo in our state. Our teachers had given strict instructions that we were to use the buddy system. Neisha, Reina, and I, together with James (the only Black boy on the trip), decided we would navigate the zoo together. None of us had been especially tight before we had boarded the buses that Monday, but by that Thursday afternoon, the trip to the plantation, one in which tour guides acted shy about admitting that enslaved people had lived and worked there, had brought us together. Apparently my endless chatter, or my inability to be as appropriately cool and detached as twelve-year-old me should have been, got on the nerves of Reina and Neisha for the last time. At some point, I turned around and they had ditched me, abandoning the buddy system and leaving me to find my way back to the bus. Looking around frantically, I spotted them several yards up ahead, snickering and giggling to themselves as they assumed they had gotten away with their mean joke. Not wanting to be lost, I followed slowly behind, keeping them in sight so that I wouldn't be late to the bus. But since they wanted to be away from me, I didn't catch up to them either. I walked along, humiliated that I needed them to find my way back and afraid to call out their behavior for fear that the friends I had finally found would no longer be my friends. I wondered what it was that

I had done to make them hate me. I arrived back at the bus
a few moments after they did, but we never spoke about how
they had left me in the middle of a "jungle" without backup.
I knew I wasn't ready to ditch them and go it alone again, so
there was no point in making a scene.

A few weeks later, apparently Neisha had reassessed her
view of me, deciding that we would in fact "need each other"
next year. Post–thirty-year-old me wishes I had had the nerve
to tell her to shove it, but I really did need her, and she really
did need me. We were overachieving Black girls in predominantly white classrooms, and what that trip to learn about
our heritage had taught us was that our story bound us together and didn't allow us the privilege of building friendships based on shared affinity and personality alone. Black
girls had to stick together.

So stick we did. We exchanged phone numbers and then
spent the summers between seventh and eighth and eighth
and ninth grades giggling on the phone endlessly, talking
about boys and having phone romances with boys that we
connected to through an endless string of three-way calls.
Two summers before, it was my white bestie, Mandy, whom
I'd called to tell when my period showed up a few days before the start of sixth grade. But sharing the secrets of growing into my Black womanhood with my white bestie, when
our social lives were increasingly racially segregated, made
for an unsustainable friendship by the end of middle school,
causing Mandy and I to grow apart. By the summer of '93,

it was my Black bestie Neisha I'd called to talk about the harrowing events of the night before, when my mother's live-in boyfriend, angry over their impending breakup, beat her, forcing me to choose between grabbing a knife and calling the police. I was thankful that I had a Black girl to call, and I realized that if circumstances had been different, I wouldn't have told Mandy at all. Neisha's family was different from mine. She had a married mama and daddy and two big brothers who lived in the house with her. Still, I felt like she would understand more. And she did. She listened and offered support. Perhaps that is why my mother, slightly embarrassed and incensed with me for telling her business, let it ride. Black girls of every age need other Black girls who can hold their truths.

I was deep in the throes, that summer, of my girlhood crush on Ronnie Groves, a nerdy Black boy who was two years older and who had beaten me in Bible Quiz at Vacation Bible School two summers prior. My head and diary were filled with hopes and wishes that he would be my first kiss. I was surprised and unprepared for the moment when I found myself fantasizing about kissing Neisha, having picked up from the ether, rather than from any particular conversation, that girls didn't kiss girls.

Up until college, I had only ever encountered one lesbian, a woman named Wendy, whom all the adults in my life seemed to like and respect and smile at when she was around, but as soon as she was out of earshot, they would whisper about how she "went the other way." Wendy rocked a Jheri Curl, drove a long green car, and always had on shades, which she wore, looking back on it, like armor. I simply thought she looked a little mysterious. She had a pretty smile and a friendly demeanor, but it was clear to me that she existed on the out-skirts of our small, tightly knit community because she was "different."

Liking girls didn't seem like a viable possibility for me. Fantasies of kissing Neisha weren't frequent, but the closer I felt to her, the more I imagined what physically expressing that closeness might look like. Thankfully (or perhaps not), my mother paid for monthly subscriptions to all the great teen magazines of the nineties: *Sassy, Teen, Seventeen,* and *YM. YM* was my fave and *Sassy,* the most feminist of them all, was my least fave. Wokeness has been a process for me. So I turned to the monthly advice columns every month and read questions that readers would write into the mag about sex.

My boyfriend and I were messing around one day and he was inside me a little bit. Am I still a virgin?

While I found that question quite scandalous, I was re-lieved when I read this question:

Sometimes I think about what it would be like to kiss another girl. Does this mean I'm gay?

"No," the columnist replied.

Your body is changing and you are having lots of feelings. It's perfectly normal in the sexual development process to fantasize about members of the same sex. But don't worry about it. You're probably not gay, and you'll figure it out in time.

The magazines worked to assure girls that they were most probably straight, subtly making it clear that queerness was not desirable. But back then, conversations about queerness and gender fluidity hadn't trickled down to my Louisiana middle school. You were one or the other, in or out, gay or straight. Relieved and assured of my straightness, I placed Neisha, my one real close Black friend, in the friend-only category and went back to crushing on cute-ass Ronnie Groves. The thing I know today, after many cycles of homegirls, many more years of girl crushes, and a life of straight sexual activity, is that one can't truly be a feminist if you don't really love women. *And* loving women deeply and unapologetically is queer as fuck. It is erotic in the way that Audre Lorde talks about eroticism. It's an opening up, a healing, a seeing and being seen. Good sex is all these things, too. My friendships with women have never been overtly sexual, but a good many of them have been what bell hooks in her book *Communion: The Female Search for Love* called romantic, in the soul-inspiring way that someone being thoughtful about loving you and showing up for you is romantic. Often those connections have what hooks called "an erotic dimension . . . that acts as an energetic force, enhancing and deepening ties." There is no room in my life for shallow or basic connections.

Feminism helped me to be okay with what it means to love women in the womanish and womanist ways that Alice Walker famously talked about—"sexually and non-sexually." These days, on what one of my homegirls has deemed #ThottieThursdays, it has become customary for my girls and I to sext one another slyly seductive pics of our asses, or thighs, or cleavages, sometimes bare, or sometimes clothed in the perfect way that all our curves are accentuated. And the tacit agreement is that we share to be affirmed, in our sexiness, in our beauty, and in our glory. When this particular group of homegirls first started with their shameless flirting and body commentary, I used to blush furiously, not knowing where this kind of engagement fit for me, a straight girl. But for this same me, who has been single, alone, and often lonely for most of my grown womanhood, ofttimes the flirtations and sexy comments from the homies are the only compliments I get.

One of the biggest battles that second-wave feminists of the seventies had with third-wave feminists of the nineties was over the place of sex and beauty in feminism. Second wavers critiqued high heels and lipstick as oppressive expectations of the patriarchy. Third-wave white girls brought heels and fly red lips back into the mix. Black feminists gave the side eye to white girls and their feminist waves, because looking fierce and fly has always been a part of the Black-girl credo. (And also because Black feminism didn't fit neatly within the historical trajectory of waves.) Our embrace of femininity was its own armor in a world where white women said that Black women should never be called ladies. If I have to pick a side, I'd say I'm second wave enough to put middle fingers up to the patriarchy and I'm third wave enough to affirm that beauty and the desire to be wanted still matter. When you go for months or years without a dude (or any love interest) ever noticing you, you can begin to feel invisible. And feminist principles about how the patriarchy has made us beholden to beauty culture do nothing to assuage the desire we all have to be seen and affirmed.

The old adage is that all feminists are lesbians. So what if that's true? Here's the thing, and there's really no straight way to say this. Black feminism is and has always been a fundamentally queer project. Straight chicks gotta make their peace with that, and hopefully without too much struggle.

I would venture to say that most tried-and-true feminist chicks are open to the possibility of their own queerness, because desire is fluid and because the boundaries and labels matter so much less when you get down to the real work of what it means to love Black women in a world that hates us all. One time, when I revealed to one of my girls that I was post-thirty but still hadn't figured out how to have an orgasm that I didn't give myself, she looked at me with a look of incredulity and thinly veiled disgust at the dudes I had slept with and said, "Shit. I'll fuck you." She was only half-joking. I didn't take her up on her offer, but I did realize that I needed to seriously invest in my own pleasure, or else I was in for a homegirl intervention of a very different sort. Deep and abiding love can be sisterly and it can be erotic, and sometimes it can be and needs to be all these things at the same damn time.

On more than one occasion, I've had a male lover say to me, upon finding out I'm a feminist, "Are you a lesbian? Are

you sure?" Rather than being reactionary and defensive, perhaps straight women need to become less invested in the
project of straightness altogether. Let me be clear. I'm not
telling you who to sleep with. I'm also not telling you that
all feminists want to or should want to sleep with women.
I am saying that far too many women leave behind the freedom feminism offers because they want to stay on patriarchy's dick, which is to say they want to secure their straightness
and their options for getting chosen.

I love a penis attached to a man who knows how to use it,
but I'm uninterested in femme-style battle royales over dick.
That's just so basic. Who has time? Feminism wouldn't be
feminism if it didn't encode a healthy skepticism about the
politics of getting dick. And feminism wouldn't be feminism
if it didn't celebrate the power of pussy. It might be trite but
it's true. To be clear, and not transphobic, feminism is also
not about the elevation of particular body parts. My transwomen comrades have taught me that you don't have to
have a vagina to have a pussy. And my lesbian homegirls
have extolled to me the virtues of the "D" their own lesbian partners are throwing down. The larger point is that
however dope fellatio may be, fellating the patriarchy is no
way to win.

If Black women don't figure out how to love other Black
women (cis and trans, queer and straight, and everything in
between), it will be the death of us. This toxic behavior of
not fully knowing how to love other Black women shaped
my earliest Black-girl friendship with Neisha, and shaped
many of my other friendships for years to come. I put up with
Neisha's mean-girl behavior almost until the end of high

school. But one summer night, after a minor spat but after many years of holding in my wounded feelings, I snapped and tried to fight her, only to have Reina hold me back. It's the first and last time I've ever come that close to letting a Black woman catch these hands. Sometimes the sisterhood hurts.

This toxicity that dogs Black women in friendships almost ruined my college friendship with Tracey, too. Inexplicably, a few months after pulling my card about feminism, she stopped talking to me. Months later, she said I had become "too intense," which I read to mean too close, too attuned, too involved, too much. The subtext, though neither of us ever spoke it out loud, was that I was doing "gay shit" and it made her uncomfortable. Perhaps I was. I never imagined kissing Tracey, never wanted to sleep with her. But I loved her, deeply, because it's the only way I know how to love Black women. I loved her because she loved me enough to check me when my feminist analysis was raggedy. But Neisha had taught me not to stay in friendships out of fear of being alone, so I endured the homegirl breakup with my chin up as much as I could, which is to say, not very much. One day my roommate Alicia came home and caught me crying big hot tears over this latest friendship failure. Yet again, I had done too much and managed to run off the closest Black friend that I had. "Sometimes, Miss Bertney, (Alicia's nickname for me), it's not that people don't love you, it's that they don't have the same capacity to love as you do. Most people are doing the best they can." Alicia's words felt wise and true, and they helped me to pick my face up and move on. Months later, Tracey apologized, saying to me, "You simply loved me, and I didn't know how to take it. I hope we can repair our friendship." Intimacy between Black women matters on its own terms, and it isn't a threat to the other kinds of relationships we want to have in our lives.

So many Black women of my generation want access to the suburban fantasy marriage more than almost anything else. All I had imagined for my personal life at age twenty was that I would get married, have three kids, and enjoy taking care of a family. It's laughable now since I don't particularly like children, unless they belong to people I love. I had nuclear-family dreams because I had bought into the notion that the way I grew up—in a single-parent home, with a mismatched family of aunties and uncles and cousins and grandparents bringing up the rear—was not optimal. So part of my success story involved having it all—the house, the car, the career, the pretty man, and the kids. It's fine to want all those things. But it's dangerous to get them in a context where you have no analysis of how and why those are your desires. Feminism helped me to think more robustly about where I had gotten the idea that my upbringing was wrong or lacking. (Moynihan was one place. The church was another. And I'll say more about both of these later.) And feminism helped me to recognize that there were other versions of a life to want.

When my patriarchal nuclear fantasy didn't happen and the privileges of straightness eluded me and a whole generation of overachieving Black women, it is my girls who have celebrated my successes, showered me with compliments, taken me out on dates, traveled the world with me, supported me through big life decisions, and showed up when disasters struck. One of feminism's biggest failures is its failure to insist that feminism is, first and foremost, about truly, deeply, and unapologetically loving women.

Beyoncé gets this lesson about feminism better than most. And she has been one of the biggest victims of this failure to love women among Black feminists. Until the release of her magnum opus, *Lemonade*, an album so self-consciously about the interior lives, struggles, and emotions of Black women that even most of Bey's haters had to bow down, I have never seen so much vitriol, particularly among Black feminist women, as I have seen in their reactions to Beyoncé. Never.

They simply didn't believe that the pretty, light-skinned, affluent, superstar Black girl could really love other Black girls. For most of us, her #prettyprivilege conjured up the mean girls we encountered at twelve and thirteen—that age when we all felt deeply misunderstood, and were prone to be mean to others while being the target of other mean girls ourselves. Of course we are no longer adolescents, but something about seeing Beyoncé shine makes that particular truth go right out the window. We could call it the defenestration of feminist common sense. It's as if the girls who were bullied finally have the chance to be the mean girls, and, where Beyoncé is concerned, they have embraced that role with gusto and absolutely no sense of irony.

Beyoncé is *my* feminist muse.

She didn't start out that way. Back in 1997, she was just one of the members in a girl group that I loved, singing the soundtrack to my senior year of high school. Three years later, when two of the original group members left, I swore that Beyoncé was the cause and refused to buy any more Destiny's Child albums. But I've always been terrible at holding a grudge, and by the time Bey dropped her first solo album during the fall of my first year of graduate school, I was back on board. Over the next decade she became Beyoncé the multi-talented mega-superstar that we know today, largely by keeping Black girls supplied with anthems for every possible life event. She was girl power personified, so I didn't necessarily need or expect her to have a critique of the patriarchy or a formal membership to the feminists club. (BTW, for all you card-pullers, no such club exists.)

By then, she was inspiring all of my best feminist theorizing. When I heard the 2006 club track "Get Me Bodied," I definitely did an "old-school dance" or two, as the song entreated, but I also thought about feminist body politics, and what it might mean for a Black girl to really get in her body, love it, and stay there. When I heard her "Upgrade U," I cringed when she sang, "I can do for you what Martin did for the people, ran by the men" (both because of the bad grammar and the even worse politics), but perked up when she said, "but the women keep the tempo." I have thought long and hard about what it means for women's bodies to keep the tempo of social movements. Some of my best academic theorization around feminism has come from pondering what kind of space Bey might be making for the particular ways in which Black women can be and can lead.

At some point, a journalist named Jane Gordon asked her directly whether she was a feminist. Many Black women musicians had been asked this question before Bey. Erykah

Badu and Queen Latifah readily come to mind. Both denied identification with the term, citing an affinity for "humanism" in Erykah's case, and a love for Black men in Latifah's. Beyoncé replied:

> *I think I am a feminist, in a way. It's not something I consciously decided I was going to be; perhaps it's because I grew up in a singing group with other women, and that was so helpful to me. It kept me out of so much trouble and out of bad relationships. My friendships with my girls are just so much a part of me that there are things I am never going to do that would upset that bond. I never want to betray that friendship because I love being a woman and I love being a friend to other women.*

When I heard Beyoncé articulate friendships with Black women as the core of what feminism was for her, it felt to me like she got the core essence of what this is all about. *I love being a woman and being a friend to other women* should be feminism's tagline. If this isn't true for you, you aren't a feminist. I'm not much on pulling people's feminist cards, but some shit we should just be able to say.

Eventually Beyoncé went on to adopt Chimamanda Adichie's position on feminism in a song called "Flawless" on her 2013 self-titled album, in which she quoted from a YouTube clip of Adichie's TED Talk: "Feminism refers to the social, political, and economic equality of women." Adichie's own failure in early 2017 to understand that transwomen are deserving of this social, political, and economic equality perhaps makes her a problematic feminist icon for many of us. When asked about transwomen, Adichie struggled, in an interview, to acknowledge that they are women. Instead, she said, "there are women, and then there are transwomen." And while it is okay to acknowledge that all kinds of women, whether white, Black, Indigenous, Latina, Asian, cis, gender nonconforming, trans, queer, bi, or straight might have different experiences, it's not cool to act as though transwomen are in some entirely separate category from the more general category of *woman*. That is something that feminism needs to be clear on—that it isn't feminism if all women's concerns, particularly the most marginalized women's concerns, aren't taken seriously.

When I think about why Beyoncé matters so much to me as a feminist, it is the first definition that always resonates, the one that she seemed hesitant to articulate, the label she seemed ambivalent about adopting. Her feminism of deeply connected relationships is one that escapes notice in our rush to make sure our feminism names every *ism* and every intersectional category in its articulation. It doesn't matter if we get the rhetoric right, though, if we still keep treating other women wrong.

Some would argue that Beyoncé hasn't helped with that. On that very same feminist track "Flawless," the chorus insists "bow down bitches" over an infectious Houston Hip Hop beat. Immediately, I watched Black feminist chicks losing their minds, citing their outrage over having someone as powerful as Beyoncé telling them to bow down. 😔 This outrage felt rooted in willful ignorance and emotional dishonesty. I'm glad that Hip Hop has always been a part of my feminist journey, because I take Joan Morgan's call for "a feminism brave enough to fuck with the grays" as bible. You can be deeply invested in loving other Black women, but still need to proclaim sometimes that bitches need to bow down. One, I don't take bitches to be gender-specific. Call that a feminist disruption of the sexism inherent in the English language. And two, if I had had Beyoncé's anthems as a twelve- or thirteen-year-old, on more than a few occasions, I might have wanted to tell Reina and Neisha to bow down.

Loving Black girls is complicated, but loving oneself in a world where there is always someone ready to do you harm is even harder. I'm not trying to resolve the contradiction of proclaiming you love Black women one day and potentially telling them to bow down the next. I'm asking us to sit with the pain and offense that make that space necessary. I'm asking us to sit with the mean-girl tendencies we all have, with the ways that we hurt each other and don't show up for each other. I'm asking us to sit with the Beyoncé conundrum that exists for all of us. At least she had the courage to own the messiness of it.

And that's why feminism needed Beyoncé. Because she has been more truthful about how hard it is for Black women to get on the same page than any of us professional feminists have ever been. After Beyoncé, feminism was no longer something reserved for Black girls with college degrees and Ph.D.'s. Suddenly feminism wasn't just the province of Black girls who'd read bell hooks. Armed with feminist narratives in the digital age, this Black girl who'd built a singing career instead of going to college could be a feminist, too. And she would use her considerable cultural power to spread the gospel of feminism to the masses.

I wasn't prepared for the ways many of my Black feminist comrades resented her for it. bell hooks, the scholar and thinker who made it possible for Black girls like me to write books like this, called Bey a "terrorist." She was responding to Bey's image on the cover of *Time* magazine, a very blond, damn-near white rendition of Bey, in which her image approximated white womanhood in ways that felt a little too close for comfort. I think hooks read Bey as flirting with whiteness and passing for white in ways that were fundamentally anti-Black and not affirming for women of color. I wish that she had said that, rather than throwing around the very loaded language of "terrorist" all willy-nilly. Another group of Black feminists got together and proclaimed Bey's feminism "bottom-bitch feminism," the kind of faux feminism that they felt accompanied the politics of sex work.

The rage was eloquent, to say the least. It spilled out in think piece after think piece after think piece, attempting to beat back the march of Beyoncé's feminism, like it was the bubonic plague come to wipe out centuries of effort from Black women activists. The rage was eloquent, but it wasn't righteous. And mostly it read as just plain wrong to me. Black women with unchecked rage and emotional work left undone can do real harm.

Our feminist origin stories matter. When I watched Black women deem this girl a *brand* instead of a human being, a stealthy rhetorical move that enabled them to distance themselves from her and then drag her for filth without compunction, it read to me like grown Black women using the power of feminism to punch down (or up) at the mean girls who they resented in childhood. I'm no therapist, but I'm a Black girl's Black girl, and I know Black-girl pain when I see it. Many of us who couldn't access pretty privilege, those of us who weren't popular or cool, those of us nerdy girls who stayed to ourselves, wrote stories and dreamed of lives as writers, grew up and found a home in feminism, a place where we were seen, a place where others were as mad about injustice as we were.

But for many of us, the first real injustices that mattered to us, that ripped our hearts out, weren't the failings of our parents' relationships, or the boys we crushed on who didn't love us, but the Black girls who we wanted to see us and befriend us instead either ignored or bullied us. I believe Bey conjures up all that shit, and that feminist analysis gives us the language to bludgeon her with our pain while feeling as if we are doing so in the cause of justice.

There is never just cause to beat a Black woman like she stole something when she is very clearly taking the pieces of her life and trying to build something magnificent. Misdirected rage is a dangerous thing . . . a deadly thing. But the power of Black feminism, of any good analytic frame, really, is in its ability to clarify what the stakes are.

What would it mean to ask the question, Why is Beyoncé drawn to feminism? If this feminist world we proclaim is so dope, why wouldn't a Black girl like her want to be part of this work, too? And if her husband Jay Z's recently released confessional album 4:44 is any indicator, perhaps feminism helped Bey find her power when she was confronted with an unfaithful partner. Feminism has certainly been a soothing reminder of my badassery every time I've been forced to mend my own broken heart.

Something about the thoughtfulness and intentionality with which she has publicly grappled with her feminist journey makes it feel authentic to me. Yes, my willingness to believe the best about Beyoncé comes from my insistence on believing the best I can about Black women. It is not a small thing to have the world's biggest pop star on our squad. There are still far too many young women who are hesitant to claim their feminism for us to be snobs about who gets to be included.

Recently, I had to stage a homegirl intervention of my own for a young sister struggling with the meaning of feminism. The young woman, a student at Howard, had emailed to ask if I would come to her research presentation on my campus. Of course, I obliged her. During her presentation about her research on Black girls, I sat brimming with pride at her professionalism but also curiosity about the conspicuous absence of Black feminist theorists from her presentation. Afterward I asked her about that choice. "Well, Dr. Cooper, I'm not sure about feminism." "Why?" I asked, even though I suspected some of what her answer might be. "It just seems like Black women are trying to force white women to accept and include them. I'm still not over how those suffragists treated Ida B. Wells at that march in 1913." She was right. A group of white suffragists had tried to force Wells to march in back during a 1913 suffrage march. Wells patently refused, though, and found a way to march with her state delegation.

As I sat and talked with the student who had far more sophisticated reasons for rejecting feminism than I had when

I was a student, I wondered yet again about why it is so easy for Black women to ignore how important feminism is to our lives. I began by reminding her of the obvious: despite white women's racism, Ida B. Wells felt she had a right to be at the suffrage march. Black women care about feminism because sexism and patriarchy affect our lives, too.

Then I shared with her some things I've learned on my journey to feminism. First, I'm not merely a feminist who happens to be Black. I'm a Black Feminist, *capital B, capital F.* That means I learned my feminism from Black women, and my feminist theory and praxis is situated in the particular ways Black women have understood, thought about, and written about the problems of racism and sexism across space and time. My feminism begins not with Susan B. Anthony and Elizabeth Cady Stanton showing out at Seneca Falls, but with Maria Stewart, a Black lady abolitionist, who was schooling audiences of men and women, Black and white, in Boston in the 1830s. When Sister Stewart asked her audience, "How long shall the fair daughters of Africa be compelled to bury their minds and talents beneath a load of iron pots and kettles?" I see in her question an insistence on prioritizing the well-being of Black women and girls. When she then steps to Black women and says, "We have been possessed of by far too mean and cowardly a disposition, though I highly disapprove of an insolent and impertinent one," I see her grappling with the ways that rage has been our constant companion. I see her challenging Black women to make that rage count. And while I think Black women have every right to an attitude problem, I get Stewart's point. She concludes by telling Black women, "Do you ask the disposition I would have you possess? . . . Sue for your rights and privileges. Know the reason you cannot attain them. Weary them with your importunities. You can but die if you make the attempt; and we shall certainly die if you do not." This is my Black feminism—the kind that is gonna channel all this rage to either get free or die trying.

Second, I have too much feminist shit to do to spend my time hating white women. Any time a white woman says something wrong in the public sphere these days, there is an army of Black feminist writers at the ready with think pieces that can snatch her wig and have her picking her face up off the floor months later. Going after white women online will get you lots of clicks and likes. But you'll feel exhausted at the end and, often, white women's attitudes won't have changed one iota. I'm not saying white women don't do treacherous shit. Far too often they are straight-up enemies to the work of ending patriarchy and racism. But we still can't let white women become the center of a conversation that *isn't about them.* I have had other Black feminists drag me (or try to) when I have said this. They have said I'm caping for white girls. Have you met me? Black feminism is not a reactionary project. It is not about the damage that white girls do. Not solely or primarily. Black feminism is about the world Black women and girls can build, if all the haters would raise up and let us get to work. When I talk about owning eloquent rage as your superpower, it comes with the clear caveat that *not everyone is worth your time or your rage.* Black feminism taught me that. My job as a Black feminist is to love Black women and girls. Period.

The third thing Black feminism taught me is that I was

once willing to let a Black nationalist–centered politic, largely narrated to me by Black men, have me put my own political needs and concerns on the back burner to center their needs and concerns. It's odd in this political moment that Black feminists resent white women more than Black men because when I think of the harms I've dealt with and who has caused the most pain, done the most emotional and physical violence, it is always always always Black men. They have done the shooting, the cheating, the beating, and the devaluing. Yet when a young Black man gets killed by police, my ass is in the street proclaiming that "Black lives matter." When Black women get killed, Black men never manage to plan such marches in solidarity with us. Though our bros ain't loyal, we insist on showing up for them. In a world where capital "B" Blackness matters as much as it does, I'm not sure that this obviously contradictory approach to our feminist politics will change. Where brothers are concerned, shit is and will always be complicated.

After laying all this out, I realized that I sounded like a feminist evangelist and that perhaps I had hemmed the girl up a little too hard. So I backed up, and simply urged the young Howardite not to leave her intellectual and political heritage at the door because of the ways white women often act. She listened to me, but she still looked skeptical as hell. I guess I deserved it for all the talking crazy I did way back when.

This is why I worry about a Black feminist politic that spends all its time tearing down Black girls who aren't deemed radical enough on the one hand and white girls and their relationship to racism on the other. Stewart didn't say we shouldn't give white folks the business. She said the opposite. But she also reminds us that Black women and girls should be at the center. My Black feminism keeps my eyes on the prize, the prize being Black women and girls. My Black feminism insists that we center them, that we talk about them, that we build a world for and with them, that we fight alongside them. Black feminist rage can change this world, but it can also destroy us if we are not careful. It's just that powerful. It's powerful because the power of a good political analysis is that it can be a masterful cloak for the emotional work we haven't done.

Look, I know the world is not Black and white. But for Black women, our relationships to white women and Black men are still the primary definers of our feminism. Being in solidarity with the Latina chick or the Asian American chick in the struggle feels not uncomplicated but sensible. It's dealing with all the feelings around white girls and black boys that get us all caught up. And in the midst of that predicament Black girls are always the compass, pointing us to the North. That is the most important lesson that Black feminism taught me. That a Black girl—my homegirl—saved my life. She did it by lovingly calling me out (or rather calling me in, as the kids say) on my bullshit. We need each other to survive.

STRONG FEMALE LEADS

I have a complicated relationship with white women. As clear as I am about needing Black women as a matter of survival, I feel far less sure about the need to be in solidarity with white women. And no other relationship causes me to reckon with that fact more than the political rise and fall of Hillary Rodham Clinton. I have been a spectator to her political career since 1992, when her husband became the first Democratic president in my lifetime. I was twelve years old when he took office, and my conflicted, complicated feelings about Hillary Clinton are deeply rooted in the very relationships with white girls that shaped my early adolescence, which happened simultaneously with her entrance on the national stage. But first, let me tell you why things with me and white girls are the way they are.

On the one hand, if my television viewing preferences are any indicator, I love white women, especially those who run shit. My Netflix queue is populated with shows that feature

"Strong Female Leads": *Gilmore Girls, The Unbreakable Kimmy Schmidt, Girlboss,* and *Grace and Frankie*. I can be found on any given day watching reruns of *Madame Secretary, Rizzoli & Isles,* or *Veep* on regular television. And Rachael Ray gets as much credit for my cooking style as anything my mother and my grandmother ever taught me. I know I just committed country Southern Black-girl blasphemy, but I long ago swapped out those delicious cans of flavor-infused, heart-clogging used grease for a bottle of EVOO (extra virgin olive oil).

On the other hand, I haven't had a white girl for a friend since 1998, the year I graduated high school. The last white girl to visit a place where I lived was my friend Michelle, who famously stepped into my room one day and put my Luster's Pink Oil Moisturizer in her blond hair and claimed it gave her texture and body. We both giggled about it, her in delight at using Black haircare products and me at the absurdity of this white girl, my friend, putting my pink oil in her white-girl hair. Real friends can share cross-cultural intimacies like that.

But until the Netflix-user algorithm clued me in, I had no idea that I had a predilection for watching white girls run the world. How can an avowed Black feminist be in love with imagined worlds in which white girls are at the center of everything?

It all started with *The Baby-Sitters Club*. Well, really, it all started with Tami Brown, a poor, mousy-brown haired white girl who could have fit the description of Ramona Quimby in Beverly Cleary's *Ramona* books, which I loved. Tami screamed the words "dirty nigger!" to me on the playground at recess. When I was eight years old, I only registered "nigger," a word I had heard my father use before among his friends, as an insult because it spewed forth from the beet-red, angry, scrunched-up face of this white girl. She delivered it with such force that my body recoiled from the shock of it, even though I wasn't fully aware what she meant. That night, I came home and asked, "Mama, what does the word 'nigger' mean?" Before my mother answered, her face winced in pain. I had never seen that look before, but I registered that she hated hearing and knowing that her daughter had been called such a thing. Mama stopped stirring the pot on the stove, looked at me intently, and replied, "An ignorant person! A nigger is an ignorant person." Tami Brown may have been ignorant, but she had just initiated me into a world of racial knowing of the worst sort.

White girls were still kind of new to me. I had only recently started spending any significant time with them socially, after my first-grade teacher discovered that I was an advanced reader. That meant I could no longer stay in my disproportionately Black, middle-ability-track elementary school classroom. I was moved to the predominantly white upper-ability classroom. Mandy, whom I met in second grade, was my best friend. She was nice to me and we ended up playing together at recess every day. Mandy invited me to skating parties and church cookouts. But then there was Tami, who looked at me as though my skin was shit-stained brown.

My newfound congress with white girls brought me great joy. One day Mandy mentioned that she was part of a cool club called the Brownies, so I came home and told my mama I wanted to be one. After having worked all day, she honored the whim of her seven-year-old, hustled back out the door, packed me into the backseat of her Chevy Chevette, and drove me over to the school cafeteria for the Brownie meeting. The school was completely dark, because her seven-year-old had the wrong location. We drove back home, dug the flyer out of the trash can, found the proper location, and then drove across town to get me all signed up for Girl Scouts. As a hardworking single mom, my mother's commitment to getting me to that meeting taught me that she was invested in my doing positive activities that would enable me to become a self-possessed and confident Black girl. She was also probably just a bit worried about whether I would make real friends given this new social world in the higher-track classes. Girl Scouts became my proper introduction to the social lives of Southern white girls, the deliciousness of s'mores, and the wonders of going to sleepaway camp.

These new friendships also alienated me from any Black friends I might have had; I quickly became the object of ridicule among my black classmates, who accused me of "acting white." I was not yet fully clear on what all the shifts in my friend demographic meant, but Tami made it plain. There was a word, an angry, hateful, stigmatizing word that named the difference between me and my new white friends.

I tried to make sense of this whole new world through the very vehicle that had brought me into contact with so much whiteness in the first place—a love of books. By the end of third grade, I had plowed through Judy Blume's Fudge series, all of the Ramona Quimby books, and every hardcover chapter book that arrived at my house from the Weekly Reader Children's Book Club. I escaped happily into fictional worlds populated by nice, adventurous, friendly white girls. I don't know that I chose these books because the girls were white. There were so few books about Black girls to choose from. The few books about Black people that I had, my aunt Colleen had boxed up and shipped to me from the Black-owned bookstore in Dallas, Texas, where she lived. A country girl in a small town, I associated access to books about my own experience with life in the big city. In the books to which I had regular access, the worlds of white girls were middle-class, nuclear, and uncomplicated, which is, fairly or unfairly, how I imagined their lives.

That spring, when the circular arrived for the book fair, I noticed one of the Baby-Sitters Club titles listed on the flyer and felt immediately drawn to it. I marked it down and asked my mom for money to buy it, along with some sticker books and other goodies at the fair. She obliged. When it came to books, my mother always obliged.

When I made it to the book fair, I beelined for book #8, *Boy-Crazy Stacey*, the first book I read in the series. Book #8 began a five-year love affair with the five thirteen-year-old Connecticut girls that comprised the BSC. Like thousands of other girls, I became a card-carrying member of the Scholastic, Inc. Baby-Sitters Club and received a real-life printed membership card and welcome packet in the mail with a letter penned by Ann M. Martin, the series author. In the fifth grade I tried to start my own baby-sitters club before I realized that I really didn't have any babies to sit and before I realized, quite frankly, that my single working mama would not take too kindly to this "venture" of mine, since it would probably amount to extra work for her. Regretfully, I reached into the makeshift loose-leaf paper "envelope" I had stapled together and refunded each girl her fifty cents in club dues.

Each month when my allowance arrived, just in time for my mother's and my monthly sojourn to the closest mall thirty miles away, I would set aside my four dollars and change to purchase the newest book in the series. I loved that it was a series, because I didn't have to let go of the characters at the end of each book.

As an only child, I considered the core members of the BSC—Kristy, Mary Anne, Claudia, Stacey, and Dawn—my friends in my head. Eventually, they took on two junior members, eleven-year-olds Mallory and Jessi. Interestingly, Jessi was African American, but I was never too pressed to read about her. I already knew what it felt like to be the only one in a friend group of white girls, and Ann Martin never quite captured that experience. But what I loved about these girls was the authenticity of their friendship. They were young, smart, and enterprising. They didn't all think alike, but they did things together. They weren't the mean girls or the cool kids, but they had their sacred friendship unit and they honored it. In the safety of that friendship unit, every girl was her full, best, awesome self. They fought sometimes, but always made up. And in the end, no matter what, they rode for each other.

I longed for that kind of close female comradeship. I craved it. As thankful as I was for sleepovers and friends to play with at school, none of my friendships ever felt like the Baby-Sitters Club. White girls for me existed in real life somewhere on a continuum from Mandy, the best of them, to Tami, the worst of them. When, in 2010, my homegirl and

I created a blogging crew called the Crunk Feminist Collective it occurred to me, after we were up and running and functioning well, that my first act in adulthood, after getting my first real job, was to basically create a Black-girl adult version of the Baby-Sitters Club! The project we undertook together wasn't baby-sitting, but the essential concept was the same—a group of young women who came together around a shared thing that we all did, to change our little corner of the world for the better. Black feminism taught me my feminism, and Hip Hop taught me my crunk, but the Baby-Sitters were the first to help me imagine what the contours of loving female friendships could look like.

These days, any show, past or present, that demonstrates authentic loving friendships between strong women (including mothers and daughters) is always at the top of my list—*Gilmore Girls, Grace and Frankie, The Sisterhood of the Traveling Pants, Sex and the City, Living Single.*

I realize now that I was mostly interested in understanding the very different lives of these older, Northern, sophisticated white girls who, because they were fictional, were different enough from the Southern white girls I knew and safe enough for me to admire and love without hurt or shame. At least that's the explanation that makes sense to thirtysomething-year-old me. What I remember is loving these fictional white girl characters, even as I learned the perils and possibilities of what it meant to live closely with white girls in real life. My Baby-Sitters Club years were populated with racial slights from the white girls I called friends. Never overt, these incidents communicated that I was mostly liked, often tolerated, but invariably *different.*

In the fourth grade, I sat at my desk one morning as my friend Candy, a member of the core group of girls I played with at recess, came around handing out invitations to her birthday party. When she came to my desk, she said, "I'm sorry I can't invite you to my party, Brittney, but my daddy doesn't like Black people." I remember how her light brown hair swung from side to side as she said it.

Later that year, when I starred in and coproduced our Black History Month play, *The Rosa Parks Story* (an idea I got from one of those Black history books Aunt Colleen had sent), Candy raised her hand first when the teacher asked for volunteers to play Martin Luther King. Her mother brought her to school with a bottle of brown makeup, which Candy smeared all over her own face. She then gave an enthusiastic rendition of King's "I Have a Dream" speech. Her mom was in the audience; her dad was not.

In fifth grade, I watched my friends and their families tie yellow ribbons on trees around town to commemorate Operation Desert Storm, the first Gulf War. A few months later, when we were all treated to the video of Rodney King being brutally beaten by four LAPD officers, no one at school mentioned it. I was left to discuss it in the blackness of my own home. In one of our deep playground conversations, which at tween ages revolved around everything from how it was to get your period to debating whether white and Black people could date, Mandy told me that her daddy said "everybody should stick with their own kind."

Still, she was my friend. Particularly in the sixth grade when she saved me in gym. We were sitting there talking about Judy Blume books, and I had just finished reading

Deenie, a book that I had gotten for a few cents on an after-noon excursion to Fran's Book Nook with my aunt Punkin, who went there regularly to restock her endless supply of romance novels. Sometimes, on her way, she would swoop by after school in her old brown 1977 Toyota Celica, pick me up, and let me ride with her. At Christmas time, when Aunt Colleen came home from the city, she and Aunt Punkin would trade romance novels.

I had also devoured and loved *Are You There God? It's Me, Margaret*, probably because as a Black girl raised in the Baptist Church, I spent a lot of time thinking about God, whether He was really as scary as the preacher said He was every Sunday, wondering whether the world really would end before I got up enough courage to get "saved," and wondering just who God was and how God thought.

Mandy was having no parts of *Deenie*. "Ew," she said when I mentioned it. "That book talks about touching your-self and stuff." "Yes, it's called *masturbation*," I said loudly to her and our friends on the top row of the bleachers. Mandy's face turned red and she ducked, telling me to keep it down. I had no idea that I had committed a cardinal teenage sin, that it was a thing to be embarrassed about, not to be discussed in mixed company. That is probably because even though I read the descriptions, I still wouldn't figure out masturbation properly until I was in college. And I didn't live in a house with older siblings who might have discussed these things. Mandy looked out for a sister that day, because getting caught talking about masturbation is only second in disaster potential to getting caught doing it.

On her birthday that year, we had a sleepover at her house

and went to the dollar movies to see *Fried Green Tomatoes*. Late that evening, upon our return, all the girls were styling each other's hair, but no one was allowed to touch mine. A cardinal rule of Black girls is that when your mama has sat up all night styling your hair, you don't let anybody else touch it. So I played in theirs, learning about the difference in textures and that you didn't need to pull a comb through a white girl's hair with nearly as much force as it took to pull a comb through a Black girl's kinks and curls.

White girls were exceedingly tender-headed, and it took me a few tries before Mandy stopped saying "Ouch, not so hard." That ability, to have a world that is centered on the prerogatives of white femininity, to command someone to stop pulling and tugging so hard upon request, is so far from the truth of so many Black girls' lives. A delicate, fine-toothed comb is no match for the average Black girl's hair. We require wide-toothed combs that are sturdy and strong and can hold our thick tresses firmly and gently at the same time, without breaking them or hurting us. For many of us are tender-headed, too. By the way, we require the same things from our lovers, our mothers, and the country in which we reside. This is not a one-comb-fits-all nation.

Before the natural hair revolution reemerged in the early 2000s and chided us for relaxing and combing the hell out of our springy, gravity-defying Black-girl hair, most of us sat between our mamas' knees and took it. We endured the endless hours of washing, detangling, drying, oiling, parting, twisting, and plaiting our hair into respectable styles so that we could look like we belonged to somebody. And it was precisely because this process took hours that we were not ever allowed to let anybody touch our hair. But the process of our mothers and aunties and big sisters and grandmothers lovingly tugging our hair into place is often the first lesson Black girls learn about the inherently tough conditions we face, about how much effort it will take to prepare us to face a waiting world, about where our safe havens are and always will be—in community with women. Who you let put their fingers in your head is sacred.

The politics of Black women's hair matters. It matters in a world where, as I learned at Mandy's party, the comb never slips through our hair quite so easily as it slips through theirs.

Later that spring, when my classmate Layla had her pool party, the great hair divide was on full display. We were in the pool in her backyard, playing Marco Polo and water tag and all manner of other games. I was under express orders not to get my hair wet, because chlorine and permed hair don't mix. As I clung to the edges of the pool, both because I couldn't swim and because I was trying to limit the amount of water that seeped inside my swim cap, my friends' mothers whispered to each other by the side of the pool, "I don't understand why it's that serious. It's just hair. Kids should just get to be kids." Of course, my mama wasn't there to defend herself because she had to work.

Still, my efforts proved futile and my hair got wet anyway. When Mama walked in under the judging eyes of the white moms hanging by the pool, I said, "I'm sorry for getting my hair wet, Mama. I tried not to." To which she replied, "We'll just have to wash it." She didn't make a big deal about it, and I was grateful, but washing and styling my hair was a several hours' long ordeal, and surely not the way my mother had intended to spend her Friday night at the end of a long week.

A few years later, another white girl friend, one with whom I exchanged notes and enjoyed a friendly classroom competition for grades, came up to me and asked, "Can I touch your hair?" Today, I would give her every side eye I have and a firm "no," but back then, I let her touch it. Her reply: "It's so soft. I thought it would feel more like a Brillo pad." Her daddy, she once whispered to me, didn't much care for Black people either.

These, though, were my friends. And this was the deep stew of Southern 1990s adolescence that shaped my own conception of girlhood. Effectively shunned by most of the other Black girls who didn't yet have the tools to understand their Black-girl magic or to make space for mine, I would have had no friends but for these white girls who invited me to sleepovers, pool parties, and the movies.

But so much of what it meant to be a Black girl among white girls, was to be a spectator and coconspirator in their construction of me as the other, as not quite like them. By escaping into the world of my beloved baby-sitter friends and later into the world of Elizabeth and Jessica, the Sweet Valley Twins, I could be a spectator and an imagined participant without risk. In this fictive world, I imagined race was only incidental and I got to revel in the shared tween and teen shenanigans of other girls, unencumbered by social difference.

To be clear, I did not fully consent to my own othering. I read every Black book my aunt sent, played with the paper dolls of Josephine Baker that arrived in one of the books, and diligently hunted for every book in Mildred Taylor's *Roll of Thunder, Hear My Cry* trilogy. On Saturday mornings, we cleaned the house while *Video Soul* and *Soul Train* played on the TV and, on lazy Saturday evenings, Luther Vandross, Johnny Gill, and Alexander O'Neal blasted from my mother's stereo system.

In sixth grade, my mama thought it would be fun to take me to my first concert. It featured MC Lyte (for me), Miki Howard (for her), David Peaston, and Surface. The Hip Hop of the nineties, which I loved, had its fair share of strong female leads, dope sistas who were kicking butt and taking names. These women were unbowed by the male-centered nature of Hip Hop culture. Hip Hop is all about loud, rowdy, and raunchy testosterone-driven narratives. These women thrived both because of and in spite of the culture. If you ask me the most memorable figures in the soundtrack to my girlhood and adolescence, my personal Hip Hop mixtape would be primarily female. My first favorite Hip Hop group was J.J. Fad, a bubblegum-pop girl group, whose 1988 hit "Supersonic" had an infectious beat that I still remember hearing for the first time as a seven-year-old in the passenger seat of my big cousin's blue Pontiac Sunbird on a country summer excursion to the corner store. J.J. Fad was gimmicky, but when I heard them for the first time, I paid attention to girls who rhymed.

For the concert my mother, who always took more interest in my appearance (thankfully) than I did, had hustled me over to Cato Fashions for an outfit. Once I reached tween age, every school year my mother would go to Cato and put a few outfits on layaway for me, so I could look fresh at the start of school. But this was a special treat. I remember that I had a cute top and these awesome baggy purple pants that felt cool and cute, and kind of like Hip Hop. I was ready when MC Lyte came out and lit up the stage.

A pioneering MC in Hip Hop, Lyte is the exemplar of a "strong female lead." She is, to this day, a confident lyricist who tells it like it is while coming off as supremely unbothered by any haters who would dare to step to her. Between Lyte, Queen Latifah, Da Brat, and, later, Lauryn Hill, Missy Elliot, Lil' Kim, and Foxy Brown, I was blessed to come of age in the era of the female emcee. Despite my lack of Black girl friends, listening to Black music, Hip Hop and R&B, made me *know* that I was a real Black girl even if none of the other Black girls around me saw it. Like Ashley Banks, the little sister on *Fresh Prince of Bel-Air*, I had a massive crush on Tevin Campbell and squealed when my mama surprised me with a cassette tape of his debut album *T.E.V.I.N.* Black girls frequently teased me for "talking white" and "acting white" but I still remember the exhilaration of seeing MC Lyte command a stage for the first time, watching Queen Latifah check sexist dudes in the "*U.N.I.T.Y.*" video, and learning all the words to Da Brat's "Funkdafied."

Most of my love of Black girl pop icons and Black music lived out of sight of anyone but my mother. That tucking away of my Black-girlness, even as I simultaneously tucked away my awareness of my friends' whiteness, was a survival skill that I honed, in part, by reading and immersing myself in the stories of white girls' lives. Before we fully learn to love ourselves, all people of color in the United States learn that we are supporting characters and spectators in the collective story of white people's lives. The stories we watch and read ask us to put aside their whiteness and relate to their very "universal" human struggles around conflict with the world, the self, and others. The problem is that only the experiences of white people are treated as universal. Meanwhile, Black movies, shows, and books are typically seen as limited and particular.

By escaping regularly into the saccharine world of fictional white girlhood, I could find respite from grappling with the enormously complicated and devastating meanings of Rodney King, Anita Hill, Clarence Thomas, and the L.A. Riots, even as all of these formative narratives about the precarity of Blackness and Black womanhood were happening around me.

And this brings me back to the moment that I, along with the rest of America, got our first taste of Bill and Hillary Clinton. When the Arkansas governor burst onto the political stage in 1992, it seemed pretty clear that there was something unique about him. His charm was then, as now, legendary.

When I wasn't in the fictive world of Stonybrook, Connecticut, or the raucous world of early nineties Hip Hop, I was devouring teen magazines. Those magazines had begun to cover a political couple from Arkansas that they referred to as "Billary." Before there were corny celebrity portmanteaus like Bennifer and Brangelina, there was Billary. But Billary was not in the least celebratory. It was a derisive dig at Hillary Clinton's political ambitions and her attempt to move away from the traditional first-lady role of being a decorous appendage to the president. I wasn't that interested in politics, but I found the wordplay clever. I watched as Hillary Clinton built a name for herself, mostly by ignoring her charismatic husband's notoriously womanizing ways. As the news of Bill Clinton's affair with Gennifer Flowers made headlines, I learned that men don't lose presidencies over cheating on their wives. Moreover, Hillary Clinton was an ambitious wife who made a failed bid for an office in the West Wing during her husband's first term. Americans admired her loyalty to her husband, almost as much as they despised her political ambitions. I also learned that if wives have the nerve to have ambitions beyond wifehood, the public chastening and disciplining is even more severe.

So much of Hillary Clinton's career in the public eye reads like a modern version of Shakespeare's *Taming of the Shrew.* Oddly enough, two of my favorite movies, both of which emerged just as Hillary Clinton ran for and won her Senate seat in New York, are remakes of *Shrew.* And I love both the white version, *10 Things I Hate About You* (1999), and the Black version, *Deliver Us From Eva* (2003). I love them because I always identified with the strong female leads at the center of these stories. Hillary Clinton's personal and professional life has been shaped by the consequences she has faced for being an ambitious and untamed woman. Though I believe she and Bill enjoy a great friendship and a political partnership, his multiple infidelities and his flaunting of them in public have certainly had the effect, if not the intent, of disciplining his wife into the role of supportive, loyal spouse. And for playing that role with aplomb, Hillary Clinton garnered the respect of many women across race and class lines. My mother told me after the Monica Lewin-sky scandal: "I like Hillary. She's handling this in such a classy way."

By that November, as the Clintons were on their way to the White House and a historic number of women on their way to Congress, the press had declared 1992 the Year of the Woman. Still, when Hillary made her failed bid for the West Wing office so she could push the agenda of universal health-care coverage, she was roundly lambasted, publicly hated, and again culturally disciplined into silence. But she put the world on notice that, as Beyoncé might say, "I'm not just his little wife." I have always lingered over stories of women who lead, women who know what they want out of this world, and women who demand that others respect them and recognize their magic.

When Hillary decided to run for president in 2008, I had initially planned to vote for her. Before my admiration for Michelle and Barack Obama and, frankly, my racial loyalty caused me to ascend the Hope train, I could think of no more qualified person to be our first female president. When again she chose to run in 2016, my fervor for her was renewed. This was despite the fact that she had called thirteen-year-old Black children "superpredators" in support of her husband's 1994 crime bill. I was thirteen when she said it, just like her daughter. And despite the fact that in 2008 she seemed to entertain the notion that someone shooting Barack Obama would put her in line for the nomination. And despite the fact that her husband made a bunch of en-titled and thinly veiled racist statements to the people of South Carolina when they backed Barack Obama in '08.

My relationship with white girls is and remains complicated. And in the public parts of my life, for good or ill,
white women's racism has never kept me from admiring
them, befriending them, or supporting them. This has been
true for multiple generations of Black women, especially
in the South. I understand Hillary Clinton at the nexus of
these competing narratives of my own womanhood and
girlhood—my complicated relationship with white women,
my innate admiration for strong women, and my hard-won
understanding of the similarities between how Black and
white communities constrict and resent women who seek
power.

The latter lesson I learned during my junior year at Howard University, when I decided to run for student-body president. Coincidentally, that was the same year that Hillary
Clinton took office as a U.S. senator. I felt that, as an overachiever my whole life and an enthusiastic joiner ever since
Mandy told me about Girl Scouts in the second grade,
running the student body was a natural progression of my
many years leading and serving in student organizations in
high school and college. Debate team, Young Lawyers Association, and Future Business Leaders.

I took this joiner sensibility right into college, where I
eagerly embraced all kinds of student associations, honors
clubs, and various positions in the expansive student government network that comprises Howard University. In my junior year, I decided that I was ready for the big time—president
of the Howard University Student Association (HUSA). Together with my running mate, Mark, I threw my hat in the
ring. At Howard, the only historically Black college located

in the nation's capital, student government campaigns are simulations of real life. Candidates spend in the thousands of dollars for fancy campaign logos and posters and splashy events to attract attention.

Naïve and idealistic, I had yet to learn at age twenty that elections are as much about popularity as about policy. In the cheerleader-jock-nerd nexus of my high school, I understood and steered clear of this. I was the girl who worked out much of what I experienced in the real world by escaping into the world of books and ideas. At Howard, no one knew the student handbook, the intercollege student government structure, or the minutiae of policies and procedures better than I did. Knowing all of these policies and procedures would equip me, I thought, to lead people.

On the day that my running mate and I went to meet with the university president, I laid out my ambitious agenda. President Swygert looked at me, as if amused, and said, "You have to get elected first." I was taken aback. I didn't fully understand the comment. It felt dismissive, condescending, and insulting. Didn't he know who I was? I had never at that point failed at any major endeavor in my life, and I didn't plan to fail at this one. Still, although it was before the age of Facebook, he had scribbled the proverbial writing on my wall.

As the election season progressed, my polling teams (yes, polling teams) would go out across the campus and canvass dorms on my behalf. They always began with two questions: Who do you think has the best command of the issues? and Who do you plan to vote for? Invariably, the response to Question One would be "Brittney and Mark." The response to Question Two would be "Stefanie and Alex," our erstwhile opponents, who would eventually emerge victorious.

Completely nonplussed by this information, I was even more taken aback by the other kinds of feedback my teams brought back with them. Students said I needed to be more feminine. I should wear stud earrings rather than my signature hoops. To this day, I only occasionally deviate from hoops. I needed to style my permed hair more effectively and wear suits and heels. I was awkward, overweight, and far more interested in books and politics than in makeup and hairstyles. I didn't even really know where to begin. Wholly naïve to the world of political campaigns, I could not understand people who thought I knew the issues better than anyone, but planned to vote for someone else. But that is what they did. Stefanie and Alex won in a landslide against us and another ticket. I should have known how it would go on election day when a known campus busybody sent a passive-aggressive message to me through one of my friends that my jeans, campaign T-shirt, and sneakers didn't "look presidential."

My spirit crushed and my eyes open to the intimate cruelty of politics, I was not a gracious loser. I did not call to congratulate the winners. I skipped class the next day, ashamed to show my failure of a face on campus, opting instead to sulk in the darkness of the movies. And I spent much of my senior year disillusioned with a campus that I felt had betrayed me despite several years of committed service.

But many of the failures were mine. Mind you, it never even occurred to me to canvass dorms with my team. The thought of soliciting strangers for votes still gives me anxiety!

(Clearly I shouldn't have been running.) It was dramatic and devastating in the way that first failures for overachievers tend to be. It was a painful opportunity to see myself through the mirror of others and find my reflection wanting. Over the course of my twenties, it became a lesson in figuring out what things about myself I would retain and what things I wanted to change. I learned first and foremost, though, that if people can't trust you, you can't lead them. Second, I learned that electoral politics weren't the thing for me. Perhaps that's petty, but living a life being evaluated by other people's impressions of me felt like too much. The third thing I learned is that it wasn't just about qualifications, or competence, or commitment, but about helping people feel connected. As a bit of an introvert and not much of a people person, I had failed to make the connection. Stefanie, my opponent, did. Students could relate to her. They found her to be genuine, rather than haughty or uptight. I was used to being one of the smartest people in the room and I acted like it, primarily as a defense mechanism.

I didn't see Hillary Clinton's loss in the 2016 election coming. Like most Americans, and most of the polling numbers, I assumed that we had arrived at a place where America was ready for a female president, especially one as hypercompetent as Clinton. In the late hours of November 8, 2016, when it became clear that she would lose, I was nothing short of heartbroken. Perhaps I should have been less optimistic.

The writing was on the wall. For more than twenty years, journalists have written essays about the reasons people hate Hillary Clinton. Every time I heard or read one of those pieces, I winced, remembering acutely how it felt to be deemed overqualified but simultaneously disliked and distrusted.

The things that made others distrust Hillary Clinton were the things that made me like her. Something about her social awkwardness, her detail-oriented policy-wonk tendencies, and her devotion to the long game of racking up qualifications through intentional résumé building feels familiar, because it is the very same strategy of every high-achieving Black woman I know. Often Black women are cast as cold and unfeeling for having these qualities. But the hustling spirit that I saw in Hillary Clinton resonated with the oft-repeated Black proverb: You have to work twice as hard to get half as far. Black women and girls are forced to navigate the unreasonably high expectations that go along with proverbs like this throughout their lives. I'll come back to that later. But I believe that there is no other group of women who can understand just how devastating Hillary Clinton's loss was than Black women. What might feel like a singular and stunning defeat for her is one that Black women learn to live with every day—the sense that you are a woman before your time, that your brilliance and talents are limited by the historical moment and the retrograde politics within that moment in which you find yourself living. Black women, from slavery to freedom, know that struggle so much more than any white person ever will.

Hillary appealed to the parts of me that care far less about impressing people than about figuring out the nuts and bolts of the kind of thinking that will actually help people. She appealed to the parts of me that despise the insincerity and superficiality of small talk. She appealed to the parts of me that come alive in intimate settings when I have the chance to connect with real people. My ability to empathize with a woman whose life and political commitments diverge significantly from my own is rooted in the ways I learned in early childhood to understand and negotiate the complex humanity of white women even before I learned to negotiate my own. I learned to like and value certain white women, despite their racism, long before I learned how to prioritize and value my own Black-girl magic.

So, yes, I think patriarchy had something to do with Hillary, whom Barack Obama called the most qualified person ever to run for the job, losing the election to a man who probably struggles to spell the word "competent." The fact that 53 percent of white women voted against her bears all the marks of the internecine ways that patriarchy pits women in an endless competition with one another. Throughout the election season, I witnessed so many white women, on both the right and the left, rolling their eyes and saying "ewwww" and "ugghh" every time Hillary Clinton came up in conversation. Somewhere in the midst of the time I spent being friends with white girls, I missed their penchant for doing mean-girl shit to each other. Everything about the ways that white women endlessly analyzed and picked Hillary apart felt like it came from the mean-girl playbook that we all learn in middle school. Perhaps it's sexist of me to reduce legitimate political analyses down to mean-girl infighting, but the political distrust and disdain for Hillary Clinton is as outsized as the vitriol that some Black feminists reserve for Beyoncé.

Look. It's not just Black and white women who I think keep replaying middle-school angst. Working-class white men's overidentification with Donald Trump, a man who clearly despises them, is the stuff of middle-school fantasy, too. Perhaps it is difficult to hear that electoral contests still are what they've always been: popularity contests. And popularity is dictated by all of the worst forms of social privilege—we are conditioned to like the people who are pretty, charming, handsome, rich, and well-connected. Donald Trump sure ain't pretty, but he is rich and well-connected, and that means that lots of white men who will never be either of these things secretly identify with him. That's all I'm saying—that so many of the emotional impulses that shape our engagements with powerful public figures have to do with the shit we went through in middle school. I really wish people would just go to therapy.

The young and woke ones on the Black left also refused to give too much credence to patriarchy's influence on the election. Many of these Black folks, some of them new and first-time voters and some of them old-school contrarians, saw Hillary Clinton as a shill for the neoliberal, establishment Democrats, a racist doing her husband's bidding, a woman unworthy of being a poster child for feminist anything. It seemed reasonable to them to protest every imperial fault of the American Republic on Hillary Clinton's back. Meanwhile, these same folks lined up behind Bernie Sanders, a socialist who had radical things to say about money, but not much else. I never believed the Bernie hype. Perhaps it's problematic identity politics, but I left white-savior narratives alone a long time ago. Bernie's Johnny-come-lately race analysis, which he hastily put together after young Black women bum-rushed him onstage at a rally, felt as opportunistic to me as Hillary's belated engagement with the politics of race. It didn't matter to me that Bernie had participated in the civil rights movement and, frankly, his close proximity to that degree of racial animus made his absence of racial analysis more than fifty years later even more egregious. Moreover, I found it especially terrible that when it came to racial politics, many young progressives, across racial lines, were far more willing to train their hatred on Hillary Clinton, a white woman, than on Bernie Sanders, a white man. White women have absolutely been accomplices to the American project of white supremacy, but their husbands, brothers, fathers, and sons have always been the masterminds. Let us never forget that.

Having grown up in a world where white women were frequently a mixed bag, I couldn't technically disagree with assessments of Clinton as a racist and a neoliberal big-money politician. My problem was that every politician on the left since Bill Clinton has been exactly this kind of politician. I didn't understand how people, knowing how patriarchy works, expected the first woman president in a deeply masculinist and patriarchal democracy to break the mold. People demanded nothing short of political purity from a woman fighting for a position in a system that has been stained bright red with the blood of countless marginalized groups from the beginning. Women are to be pure and unsullied, maternal, nurturing, and the conscience of the Republic. Clinton was maternal to her one child only, and not much interested in any of those other qualities. And many Americans, including the young of all races who have grown up with patriarchal expectations as barely detectable background noise, hated Clinton for all the ways in which she did not conform to these dictates. At the same time, a curious thing was happening among young Black feminists and progressives, who hated Hillary Clinton because she was entirely *too* white. These folks focused on her race and class politics exhaustively, and treated her gender and her long life as a woman in politics as though it were incidental rather than central to the narrative.

Even before I embraced feminism, the Howard campus election taught me that patriarchy is always on its job. Other things like race, class, and sexual orientation, might be central. But gender always matters. The angst I felt over being deemed simultaneously too good and not good enough set me on the path to feminism. For the first time, on a campus that was committed to all Black everything, I ran headlong into the politics of gender. Yes, my opponent, a woman, won. But in addition to her clear talent for politics and her doing an admittedly really great job as student body president, she also met respectable standards of femininity that I hadn't even truly been aware existed. On the day of the campus election, she wore a dark-colored suit and heels. I had no knowledge of the social mores of "looking presidential." Never before had my clothing and appearance been policed in this way, other than by my mother. My insistence on a uniform of jeans and tennis shoes was, I'm sure, a subconscious rebellion against this very same mother who, to this day, owns neither a pair of jeans nor a pair of sneakers. Never before had I encountered a world where the merit of my ideas didn't rule the day. Even in high school, though top grades and impressive college admissions didn't protect me from racism, the racists did not win. Never before had I been made to care so much about how my existence and manner of moving through the world made other people feel.

I wrote my first ever op-ed about my experience for the campus newspaper. Before Rebecca Solnit gifted us the term "mansplaining," several brothers approached me on campus, having read my article, wanting to know how the demand that I wear lipstick and smaller earrings was any different from the unspoken edict that they shave their cornrows or locs. True enough, Howard, like many other Black colleges, had (and has) a culture of respectability when it comes to what constitutes professional attire. The politics of respectability is predicated on extremely conservative ideas about what a proper race man and a proper race woman are and should look like. I watched, over the course of four years, as many young men in the School of Business cut their dreadlocks just in time for senior year and the waiting job market. Still, I offered every brother that stepped to me a withering glare and asked, "Do you really think this is the same thing?" The stakes weren't the same. Respectability politics rooted in sexist ideas suggested that I wasn't qualified to be president because I wasn't feminine enough and was not enough of a lady. Because my male colleagues were straight men, their masculinity was not called into question. No one had said that they weren't masculine enough to be president. I didn't have the language for that then.

My lack of answers to these questions left me with a sinking feeling in my gut that even though I was more than halfway through college, I didn't have even half of the answers I needed about my life as a Black woman. I wasn't a feminist yet, but my unquestioned commitment to a race-only politic was like sand slowly slipping through the fingers of my tightly clenched Black-power fist.

I also never questioned my femininity because, even though I've never been hyperfeminine, I am most at home in the company of other women. Ever since the days of Girl Scouts and the Baby-Sitters Club, I have been a girl's girl. My understanding of my girlhood and my womanhood has always been forged in relationship to other women and girls, black and white. At Howard, I ran squarely up against the intersection of race and gender, racism and sexism, in ways that I could not foresee. The kind of Black womanhood that Howard valued in its leaders during my time there in the early 2000s was a womanhood different from my own. Opinionated, outspoken, and far too serious, I didn't temper my mouth with cute hairstyles or clothes. I didn't know I needed to.

White women taught me about racism; Black institutions, like Howard and the Black Church, gave me a primer on sexism. My relationship to both are, consequently, complicated. Of course white women weren't my only examples of strong female leads. My life had been intimately shaped by strong women leading. In the intimate world that shaped me, Black women—my grandmother, my mother, and my three aunts—ran everything. They cooked the meals, worked the jobs, paid the bills, managed the kids, extinguished fires, told off racist teachers, and put out bad lovers; parted, greased, and plaited hair every night and every morning;

sewed, washed, and ironed clothes; taught us to pray, picked a mean switch for a good whuppin; and drew the boundaries of every Black child's world with a simple look. But the world of girls and women outside my home was white. In graduate school I read the Combahee River Collective, a group of Black feminist activists from the 1970s who gave me a new understanding of "identity politics," a term they invented. I had learned early how to *disidentify* with whiteness but never fully how to inhabit, embrace, and identify with my particular Black-girl magic. They argued in their famous "Black Feminist Statement," written in 1977, that "our politics evolve from a healthy love for ourselves, our sisters and our community which allows us to continue our struggle and work." So they adopted what they called "identity politics," a belief that "the most profound and potentially radical politics come directly out of our own identity." These politics of identity were radically different from the dis-identity politics that had shaped my youth. These were Black women speaking a language of liberation, of self-possession, that I didn't even know I needed.

I like strong female leads, Black and white alike. I want to be strong. Badass women have to be strong. But I don't ever want to be strong in ways that are inauthentic, dishonest, and dangerous to my health and well-being. Black feminism taught me that in the battle with white women over racism and with Black men over sexism, I can never go wrong in picking myself. But I'm grown and I know the choices are never so black and white. I love, embrace, and keep company with Black men who have yet to fully or even remotely reckon with their sexism, because those Black men are my father figures, brothers, cousins, friends, and lovers. Similarly, I can, in limited instances, admire and offer support to white women who have not yet fully reckoned with their racism. I can also admit that the struggle to take down the patriarchy will be a very limited endeavor if white women aren't a part of it. I do wish white feminists would embrace the notion, however, that in this new feminist movement we are all trying to build, they aren't automatically our choice for "strong female lead."

THE SMARTEST MAN
I NEVER KNEW

Every time I hear calls from young radical activists to "burn it all down and start again," I feel more fear and distress than possibility. While there are a fair number of Black women across history who have believed in revolutionary violence, the posture of burning shit down feels decidedly masculinist to me. Our nation's story is one of men using violence—against Native folks, against Black folks, and against women—to build and fund a grand "experiment in democracy." Very often, when we think about the way the United States likes to wield its "big stick" abroad, through military might, we forget that this project is inherently phallic. Picking on countries full of people of color with less money and resources is also a racist and imperial project. Lots of young activists of color that I know point to this. They point to the way police occupy Black communities like our military forces occupy places abroad. But militarism isn't just racist. It's also patriarchal, sexist, and masculinist. Far too many Black men crib from this same playbook, believing setting fire to white men's institutions while laying claim to land and women is what freedom looks like.

My mother's father was a military man, a World War II vet. For many black men, joining the military was their only viable option to make something of themselves in a world where they couldn't finish school and couldn't go on to college. The men in my family lived down South, the place from which other Black people fled during the Great Migration. There were no good factory jobs in these rural small towns near the Mississippi Delta to create economic opportunity for those who didn't go North. The military provided a salary and a pension. It also provided an avenue for Black men to become the kind of normative, proud, self-supporting men that are valorized in a patriarchy. In my grandfather's case, his time in the military also gave him bragging rights. According to the big white leather family Bible that sat on the coffee table next to my grandmother's weekly subscription to *Jet* magazine, Grandfather Henry saw action at Normandy. He came back from the war with an injury that he lived with until his death twenty-five years later. At some point, after he returned from the war, he married my grandmother, a young woman sixteen years his junior. Depending on who tells the story, my grandfather's personality had many faces. My mother's older sisters remember him as a mischievous and fun-loving father who piled them all into the pickup truck and took them down to the jook joint, leaving them to play in the truck for hours while he went in and gambled with his friends. My grandmother told me stories of the fights they'd have, most likely after he came back drunk from the jook. "Yes, I fought him," she'd say, reveling in her ability to stand toe-to-toe with her man. But she also spoke of the PTSD he carried. "Cooper (which is what she called him), could not sleep on white sheets. My God, he would carry on if I ever tried to make him sleep on white sheets." One can only imagine the horrors those white sheets conjured for a WWII vet born in 1911. My mother, the baby of the family, remembered her father in his old age as a gentle giant with huge hands that she'd hold as they walked around the yard to "help him get his exercise."

It's not too far a leap to think that her love for her own father, a volatile but loving family man, shaped the kinds of men my mother came to love when she was grown enough or thought she was. Bob was also a military man, several years older, tall, dark, handsome, charming, and gentle. Just the kind of man that makes mothers scared for their daughters. My grandmother warned my mother away, telling her that Bob was "no good" for her. As is the custom of daughters, my mother thought my grandmother didn't know what she was talking about.

So Mama let Bob shoot his shot. She obliged him, and things went along like a dream until, as she mentioned later, in that way that Black women can say everything while saying so little: "He didn't treat me right." As a younger woman, I wanted to know what that meant. As a grown woman who's lived a little bit of life, the broad outlines feel clear. The details matter less. My mother, a pretty, charming, smart, and ambitious girl in her first year of college, left Bob and pursued her bliss. At eighteen her bliss was another older man, himself home from a stint in the military. Charming and smart, Mann swiftly took up the space Bob had left. Bob, a Vietnam vet who would later tell my mother that his "head was all screwed up from the War," viewed it as a betrayal of the sort that deserved retribution.

On a Saturday afternoon in March, Bob came upon my mother and Mann sitting in a car across the street from Big Mama's (Mann's mother's) house. A young woman from the neighborhood would later tell my mother that she saw Bob coming and ran toward the car, waving her arms wildly in the rearview mirror, trying to get my mother's attention. Mann somehow saw Bob coming and gestured for his nine-year-old nephew David to go into the house. David heard a *pop, pop, pop* as soon as he made it inside the door. Outside, Bob shot my mother three times and Mann once.

My mother awoke in the hospital to her older sister Linda asking her if she knew where she was and whether she understood what had happened. Mama had blocked out the shooting, but she knew enough to tell her sister "Bob shot me." In the manner of rural Southern boys, my mother's big brother had ridden around all night with a shotgun and a willingness to kill. Bob called, wanting to know if my mother was alive. Lil' Mama, my mother's grandmother, simply said to my mother as she lay in the hospital bed fighting for her life, "Baby, you didn't do nothing wrong."

It has been nearly thirty-eight years since a grown man, drunk on his own sense of entitlement, attempted to murder my mother. According to several years of reports by the Violence Policy Center, in this, the second decade of the twenty-first century, eight Black women per week, more than one per day, are murdered, usually with guns, and usually by a Black male they know. More than one thousand women of all races are murdered each year, in similar incidents, usually by men of their own race. It has been said before, but it is worth saying again: Toxic masculinity kills.

At eighteen years old and in good health, my mother, thankfully, recovered. A few weeks later, she found out that she was pregnant, with Mann's baby. With me. The first time she heard my heartbeat, big and strong, she felt like she was floating on air, renewed in her decision to bring her pregnancy to term. All three of us—my mother, my father, and me—had survived the shooting. Put another way, we had survived a Black man attempting to murder us.

Because my mother now had a baby to support, she did not return to college for her sophomore year. She recovered from the shooting, gave birth to me in late 1980, and started her career at a local company at the beginning of 1981. My father struggled, using alcohol to medicate his pain and trauma, in the same way that his father—my grandfather Claudie, also known as Big Daddy—had done. On weekends, Mann got drunk and came home to fight my mother. Many years after his passing, his sister—my aunt Mattie—told me, "He loved your mother. That was the only way he knew to show it. That was all he'd ever seen." Inadvertently, she had revealed something of the dynamics between Big Mama and Big Daddy, dynamics that I had been oblivious to as a child, because I knew Big Daddy only as the lovable town drunk. I saw him far more frequently posted up under a tree, in the projects, with a brown paper bag in his pocket, than I ever saw him at Big Mama's house. I call it her house because I never remember seeing him there. And whenever I ran into him, Big Daddy always gave me the biggest smile, happy to see me. Many of my friends and I, with grandparents who grew up in the aftermath of World War II, repeat to each other the stories our parents handed down to us in hushed voices, of how *their* parents got drunk and caroused all weekend, and then came home and took their anxieties, fears, and frustrations out on each other. The women sometimes got brutally beaten or killed, but sometimes they gave as good as they got.

This had been the script of both my grandfathers, Henry and Claudie. It was the script my mother had to work with when she chose whom to love. It was the script of both of the men she loved as a young woman. Of my father, my mother has said, "Your dad and I would work all week trying to build something. And then in one weekend, he could go out and destroy everything we had worked that week to build." This is the father I remember, the weekend bringer of chaos and destruction, not the faithful, sober builder who showed up Monday through Friday, not the man who my mother made ride shotgun with her to drop me off each morning at daycare because I cried too much when she left me.

Men aren't born destroyers. Many men imbibe scripts of toxic masculinity almost from birth. And on their way to becoming men, they enact those toxic scripts in the lives of the women around them. It's important to remember that this conclusion is not inevitable. But that's the thing that will drive you mad when you lose someone tragically—wondering about the inevitability of the outcome.

It was a Saturday morning on the fourteenth of April, at around 5:00 A.M., when the phone rang in our house. It was exactly ten years and two weeks after Bob had shot my parents. I heard my mama on the phone saying, "How am I gonna tell this girl . . . ?" I knew something bad had happened, but didn't know what or to whom. Ever the straight shooter, my mama asked me to get up, and when we sat down in the living room, she said simply, "Somebody shot and killed your dad last night." I was in the fourth grade, and by that time I was well acquainted with my daddy being shot. He had been shot when I was in the second grade, and again when I was in the third grade. Both of those times, and the time with Bob, he had survived. This time, he had not. I sat on the sofa, digging my toes into our bright blue carpet, shaking my head, trying to make sense of the senseless. "We should get over to Big Mama's house. She's not doing too well," my mom said. We got dressed hurriedly, climbed in the car, and drove the couple of miles down the road to Big Mama's house.

Inside, Big Mama's face was racked with grief, and she kind of rocked from side to side. Aunt Lil', my daddy's baby sister, was distraught. "Mann never liked Friday the thirteenth. He never did," she was saying to no one in particular. But, apparently, my daddy had violated one of his own edicts by being out of the house on that Friday night. Over the weeks and years to come, a few more bits and pieces of the story would trickle in. My daddy had been at his girlfriend's house. A man—perhaps the landlord, perhaps a former lover—came by angry about money, waving a gun around, threatening her and her children. My daddy intervened and ended up dead, shot in the head. For the second time, my daddy had become the victim of another man's vendetta against the special woman in his life.

Each and every time men try to deflect conversations about intimate partner violence in Black communities by talking about how "men are victims of abuse, too," I want to hit them myself. Patriarchy and toxic masculinity (together with alcoholism and militarism) turned my father into a violent man. But patriarchy also killed him.

In the nine shared years of our story together, years framed entirely by the gratuitous violence of men, I struggled to know this man, my father, this mischievous brother called "Mann" by his family, who was a bit superstitious, a bit of a romantic, a wild dancer, and a man willing to take a bullet more than once for a woman he loved. The father I knew harassed and terrorized my mother and me. He regularly upended and disrupted our lives, demanding much but giving little. The man I knew as my dad did not square in any way with the Mann who was beloved by his family.

In the eighth grade, my substitute teacher, Mr. Roebuck, happened to be a good friend of my mother's and a minor local celebrity who deejayed at the local radio station. Soul Roe was his DJ name. In that way that Southern Black people have with each other, I went up to him after class and said, "I think you know my mother." And like Black Southerners are wont to do, Mr. Roebuck scaffolded me into a whole local genealogy, assessing, rather quickly, "who my people were." "I knew your daddy, too," he told me. I had no idea what he might say next, because I couldn't imagine what good thing he might have to say about my daddy. "He was a *really* smart guy," Mr. Roebuck told me, to my great surprise. "I saw him walking down the street one day and gave him a ride. He talked to me about starving children in Africa and all kinds of things, not the kind of things you would think a cat walking along the side of the road would be thinking about." I had heard my father's sisters' stories, about how he was smart as a whip, about how he did Lil's homework, about how he never had to study for tests. I've never met a test I didn't have to study for. But other people outside the family thought my dad, the same man who had come late one night and slashed all the tires on my mother's car, was smart. Like *really smart*, to the point that it was worth remarking on. Mr. Roebuck was subbing in my gifted and talented class, and for the first time, he introduced me to the idea that my daddy might have bequeathed to me more than grief, that my father, and not just my mother, might have had something to do with the precocity and intelligence that everyone in my family bragged on me for having.

Several months after my conversation with Mr. Roebuck, I tumbled back into grief, unable, as had I been able to do at age nine, to tuck in the fear of violence and death that were the natural aftermath of losing a parent. I could not reconcile the thoughtful, empathetic man that Mr. Roebuck had picked up along the side of the road with the man who used to ring our old green rotary phone incessantly, making it impossible to spend an evening at home in peace. The man Soul Roe knew, who had empathy and concern for everybody else's children—Africa's children, his girlfriend's children— didn't seem to have any empathy or tangible concern for his own daughter.

My father wanted me to know him. Well acquainted with his violence, I felt I knew him as much as I would ever need to know him. After an evening of drunken reveling, it was customary for him to call and demand that my mother "put Brittney on the phone." "She doesn't want to talk to you, Mann," my mother would say while I shook my head. Listening from the other end, I'd hear "No, I haven't turned her against you." And after he refused to hang up, "Here," Mama would say, handing me the phone, "talk to your daddy." "Why don't you want to talk to me?" he'd ask, hoping I would provide some evidence of my mother's campaign to "turn me against him." There had been no such campaigns. "Because you hurt Mama," I'd say. "Do you love me?" Daddy asked me once. "No, because you hurt Mama." I didn't even think twice about telling my daddy I didn't love him. How could I love him? I'd seen him inflict pain with my own two eyes. Small and powerless, I'd heard him slamming my mother into doors, even while I screamed and cried from the other room for him to stop. "Well, I love you," he said, sounding quite sober. Then he demanded that my mother drop me off to spend the day with him so that I would know him. That day he gave me as much peanut butter and jelly mixed together in a green bowl as I wanted to eat. When my mother came to pick me up, he didn't fight her. But other times, he did. Seeing me was frequently a pretext for seeing her. But people are never the sum total of the wrongs that they do. Men aren't born monsters.

The only time I ever thought I loved my dad was when I went to see him one of the times after he'd been shot. He was walking around with a cane, sober and genuinely happy to see me. He smiled and I smiled back, these smiles and faces mirror images of each other. On the ride back home, I told Mama, "Maybe I love my daddy." She said nothing. Her position on my dad was always that everything regarding him was better left unsaid. She left me to form my own opinions. I don't remember whether it was the second-grade shooting or the third-grade shooting (that's how I mark the time) when he got shot, as my mother told me, "in the lower stomach." Years later, my aunt Mattie clarified that one of his testicles had been shot off. But she told me my dad had attended the court date for the shooter. During his remarks to the judge, Daddy said, "Don't lock him up. I wouldn't wish that on my worst enemy." There was that radical empathy again, that fairly sophisticated sense that locking up a man for a drunken street fight that had gotten out of control didn't, in fact, constitute justice. Losing a testicle, my dad had suffered a violent and material blow to his own masculinity, but still he didn't equate carceral solutions with justice.

At thirteen, four years after the gun finally won and Mr. Roebuck disrupted my particular memories of my father as mostly a monster, these competing narratives bubbled over, haunting me each night. My mother made a way, despite limited income, to put me in therapy. Twice a week, the summer after eighth grade, I would go to sit on the sofa with Dr. Rick, a middle-aged white man with glasses, a beard, and a long chin. At some point, Dr. Rick assessed that the cause of my anger, the thing keeping me up nights and making me anxious, was that I needed to know my father better. The few good memories of my father that I have—the time he walked me to the store and bought me Bubble Yum, or the time he sat me on his shoulders and took me for a walk while he whistled a tune—had been overshadowed by all the negative memories. Dr. Rick sent me on a fact-finding mission to gather pictures of my dad (which I didn't have), and to figure out some of my dad's story. Talking to family friends, I started to put the pieces together, trying to connect the version of the story that I had to the version of the story that others told.

Aunt Mattie, my dad's oldest sister and the keeper of the family history, happily welcomed me for a visit, armed with old pictures, letters, and stories. In a letter dated "24 March '75," my dad wrote to her, from his post in Germany:

This is a beautiful place over here. I seen towns sitting on top of mountains and towns sitting way down in the valley under the mountains.

After checking in on everyone in the family and sending his hellos, my dad, at eighteen, mischievously concludes,

Have you seen Margie yet. When you see her tell her to write and tell Patricia to write. I don't care if she is engaged. (smile)

And he signs it,

Bye now from your BIG LITTLE BROTHER.

At thirteen, the beautiful turn of phrase and the imagery of my dad sitting in Germany, perhaps on a mountainside somewhere as I imagined it back then, thinking about the bits of world he'd seen, stuck with me. Years later, he would affectionately refer to my mother as "Schatzi," the German word for "treasure" or "sweetheart."

During my first year as a professor, I traveled to Heidelberg, Germany, for a conference called "Toward an International History of Lynching." I was giving a paper about Ida B. Wells's antilynching work, reflecting on Black women's long history of standing up to the United States for the wars it has waged on Black people, and on Black men in particular. Sitting in the window seat as the plane descended into Germany, I marveled at the beautiful, idyllic towns sitting on top of verdant green mountains, and looked curiously off in the distance at other towns tucked in the valleys below. For a brief moment, I got to see the world through my daddy's eyes.

I remember all the gifts my daddy ever gave to me: two fancy yellow bows with ribbons for my hair, a green purse for my fourth birthday, two half-dollar coins that I still have. And a picture of my sister, his other daughter, whom I didn't meet until adulthood. This momentary glimpse of his view of the world—when he was still young and excited about what was possible—felt like an inheritance, like a part of my story, whose provenance I could verify. My dad didn't leave a will, but through this letter I inherited a slice of beauty, a slice of his joy, before being a Black boy in a world that hated Black boys hardened his heart and limited his capacity for kindness.

❦ ❦ ❦

I am always struck by the ways other people's stories about my father tend to highlight his empathy and kindness for others. I wonder about a world in which you can be kind to everyone but the people who belong to you. And, in that regard, my father's capacity for empathy for the "starving children of Africa" reflects this conundrum of American empathy. On the one hand, my father had a deep thoughtfulness that I would not necessarily assume he would have as a Black man from semirural Louisiana. At the same time, he cared more for these Black children abroad than he cared for his own children, whom he never financially or emotionally supported.

In the spring of 2014, the Nigerian rebel group Boko Haram kidnapped more than two hundred school girls in Chibok and absconded with them to an obscure and impenetrable part of the country, where they would no doubt be coerced into being wives for the male rebels. On social media #BringBackOurGirls trended and then President Obama offered aid to the Nigerian government. Michelle Obama tweeted a picture of herself holding a sign that said "#Bring BackOurGirls." While Black women in the States organized solidarity actions like "Rock a Gele for Our Girls," folks on the left began to bellyache about the perils of U.S. military intervention. Many Black men argued that intervening would be militarist and imperialist, and that the woke position of any of us committed to radical politics should of course be against U.S. military intervention. Many on the left had hoped that the Obama years would bring less rather than more U.S.

military incursions abroad. U.S. imperialism is a uniquely troubling evil, even in these days of a waning empire. And as the argument went among some Black men on the left, even two hundred-plus kidnapped, raped, and forcefully impregnated Black teen girls did not warrant U.S. military intervention.

In the months prior to the kidnapping of the Chibok girls, President Obama had launched his My Brother's Keeper initiative, which was aimed at creating mentorship programs and leadership opportunities solely for young boys of color. Enraged that he would leave Black girls out of his signature racial justice initiative, I joined other Black women in organizing an open letter to the president, calling him out on his exclusion of Black girls. If our president, a self-proclaimed feminist who lived in the White House with three generations of Black women, couldn't bring himself to use his pulpit to fight for Black women, then all hope felt lost.

Are Black girls ever worth fighting for? I wonder this sometimes as a feminist who still secretly hopes for a man who will fight for her honor. I wonder this, more specifically, as a fat feminist who has been in one too many rooms where brothers have gone on the attack, misreading my large body as unduly aggressive, often resorting to using their own bodies as physical intimidation, only to have other men in the room do and say nothing. It has never been fully clear to me whether I was left on my own out of resentment, passivity, or some twisted belief that it would be sexist to stand up for a feminist, especially a physically large one who seems infinitely capable of defending herself. I have learned to defend myself because I've never been able to rely on a man to do it for me. That doesn't mean I've never wanted a man to do it for me. It strikes me that if my daddy had lived, he might have cared deeply about the Chibok girls. The fact of his empathy is no guarantee that he would have figured out how to care for and father his own daughters any better than he did when we were children.

One of my all-time favorite quotes, one that has largely been attributed to civil rights preaching luminary Rev. Vernon Johns is, "If you see a good fight, get in it." Is the fight for the lives, safety, and sense of well-being of Black girls a good fight? I think so. Does it have to be a violent fight? I hope not. But far too many brothers have walked away from the fight for Black women's lives, citing lack of interest, lack of urgency, or dogma. The feelings of disinterest and the faulty belief that Black girls aren't engaged in an urgent struggle for their lives infuriates but does not surprise me. Sexism, like every other "ism," is a willful refusal to not see what is right in front of you.

The dogmatic commitment to *not* fighting for Black women and girls confounds me. On principle, many in Black communities believe that there is never a compelling reason to stand up in unequivocal defense of Black girls. Though patriarchy is clearly a structural problem, often there is a refusal to confront it, because to do so makes it seem like Black women are "picking on" Black men. Naming the terrible things Black men have done to Black women gets too frequently read as man-bashing and hatred. But as I have said before, "We can neither heal nor fix that which we will not confront." Dogma isn't just dangerous. It's deadly. Our politics and beliefs should serve us; we should not serve them. Now I know that this position is also dangerous. I'm not advocating for a self-serving, navel-gazing politic that bends and shifts for our convenience. I'm advocating for people-centered politics that hold the safety and protection of the least of these—among them Black women and girls—as a value worth fighting for. I'm asking what it will take to have a politics that puts Black women and girls (cis, trans, and everything in between) at the center and keeps them safe. What does that look like? Because I sure as hell know what it doesn't look like.

When the Chibok girls were kidnapped, I wanted our Black president to use the force and resources of the U.S. military to go in there and bring our girls back. I wanted this same president to use the bully pulpit granted to him by the American people to proclaim that Black Lives Matter and, more specifically, the lives of Black women and girls matter. He struggled to do any of this, only coming around to cite the myriad contributions of Black women in a speech given in the fall of 2015. Those leftist radical pontificators who reside in a utopian place I like to call "Wokeland" called my position—this desire and advocacy for intervention on the part of Black women—imperialist. Black womanhood is not a politically pure category by any stretch. Any evil act we can think of, we can of course find some Black woman who has committed it.

But, structurally, it is absolutely untenable to suggest that Black women are imperialists and colonizers. In the context of the United States, our reproductive capacities were conscripted to build the capital base for the assertion of the U.S. empire. After slavery, our bodies and the children they produced were tethered to multiple generations of low-wage work and poverty, providing staffing for the perpetuation of the U.S. underclass. The desire for protection and safety is not an imperial desire. Asking the leaders of your country and the members of your race to fight for you (if you're Black) is not a colonizing act. They are demands for recognition of citizenship and humanity.

Black women know intimately what the process of U.S. militarism does to Black men . . . what military-style policing does to Black communities. We know what it means for the military to become the only viable option that so many of our people have had for access into the middle class. Every opportunity I get, I stridently discourage the young men in my family from treating the military as their pathway out. Far too often, in these days of endless war and in wars past, it sends or has sent back to us men with war raging in their hearts and ringing in their ears. Those men, who cannot cut through the madness of the violence they've seen and in which they've been forced to engage, see Black girls and women as targets—as objects for violent sexual release, as punching bags, as emotional chopping blocks.

When I was five, Bob came back. He had spent a few years in prison for his crimes against my parents. We were leaving Grandmother's house when Rebo, my grandmother's first cousin, flagged us down to say that "Bob is out, and he's been looking for you." A few minutes later, Bob drove past, recognized my mother, and pulled over, waving her to his car. Rebo, who was more like an aunt to my mother and her siblings, looked nervous and my mama looked shook. She said nothing, but then she didn't have to. Five-year-olds understand brute emotions like fear. I didn't know who Bob was or why it felt so cloudy and dark in the car when the sun was shining so brightly outside. I didn't ask questions, though. By then, my own father had caused enough chaos for me to know what danger looked, smelled, and felt like.

Frantically, my mother rushed back to town and drove directly to Cherry's Gun Shop. Inside Cherry's, a young white woman behind the counter showed my mother a small handgun. "It's two-fifty," she said. My mom just shook her head, piled me into the car, and took me home while she actively figured out plan B.

By the time we made it the couple of miles to our place in the projects, she had arranged for me to go to my next-door neighbor's, to stay with my bestie, Lawrence, and his parents. Before she left, she kneeled in the front yard so that we were eye to eye and told me, "Bob is a bad man. I'm going to the courthouse to see the judge so he can't bother me." I nodded. My mother has always had a policy of radical honesty with me, even when I was too young to understand all the ins and outs. I went inside to play with Lawrence, hoping that the judge could do something to keep the bad man away.

What does it mean to build a world in which Black women and Black girls are safe? Jail clearly didn't keep Bob away from my mother and me, and the restraining order didn't keep him away forever, either. Moreover, despite my desire for Barack Obama to send our troops to rescue the Chibok girls, the U.S. military apparatus causes harm both at home and abroad. Black men often parrot this logic of the U.S. nation-state, engaging either in the politics of doing harm or the politics of doing nothing. And we—Black girls, Black women—are not saved.

How, then, shall we live? What do Black men, who have in the aggregate been the purveyors of so much harm, owe to Black women? Black men took those Black girls in Chibok. Black on different terms than we understand Black manhood in the United States, but Black men nonetheless. That is why it felt so egregious to hear radical, progressive Black men in the United States talk about all the reasons why those little girls were not worthy of U.S. intervention. A Black man shot my mother. Four different Black men shot my father. One of those Black men killed him. Two different Black men put their hands on my mother. One of those men was my father.

I'm a Black girl, a grown Black girl, who wants the men in my life, and men who are bystanders in critical moments, to fight for my honor. I want them to have the protective impulse that my mother's big brother had the night she was almost killed. I want men to have the impulse my uncle Carl Lee, my daddy's brother, had the afternoon that he chased Daddy around the living room to stop him from putting hands on my mother. My uncle Carl Lee reminds me of the character Carl Lee Hailey in the movie *A Time to Kill*: When two white racists in Mississippi kidnapped and raped Carl Lee's beautiful little girl, that Black man took his shotgun and took them out. I've seen enough gun violence not to actually desire men to act this way, but I appreciated his moral clarity. They had harmed his daughter and thrown her in a ditch to die as though she were disposable. He had to take them out. I want Black men to feel that impulse of protection for Black girls everywhere, even when those Black girls aren't their daughters, but especially when they are.

I'm a Black woman who wants to live in a nation that believes it has a responsibility to Black women, as citizens and as people, to make the world safe for them. I'm a Black feminist who cannot reconcile my desire for men to fight for my honor with my general abhorrence for violence. I'm a feminist who cannot reconcile my desire for U.S. military intervention in Chibok with my utter hatred of guns. I'm a feminist who cannot reconcile my desire for my nation-state to intervene on my behalf with the woke analysis feminism has bequeathed me about the perils of getting in bed at any level with the logics of patriarchy and militarism. For these things might protect you one minute and kill you the next. I am my mother's daughter, and I have been taught always, *always* to stand up and fight honorably for myself. I am also the daughter of my father, Mann, who brought more relief in his absence than with his presence, who taught me that there was more security in his leaving than in his staying, a man whose lack of respect for boundaries made me chronically afraid at levels that were no less nerve-racking than the acuteness of the fear Bob induced.

Now I am a grown woman trying to build a life where I can get in bed every night with a man who knows that my desire for him to hold me down does not in any guise mean that I want him to put his foot on my neck. I am a grown woman who feels like these obvious things have to be said explicitly. I am too afraid to say these things that need to be said, because the consequence of my demands might be another man leaving me, and my father taught me that my needs weren't compelling enough to make a man stay. I am, then, a grown woman who struggles mightily to trust what it might mean for a man to stay, to show up, to catch me when I fall, acquainted as I am with the relief that comes when they finally, simply, go. The leaving feels like the tanks are finally pulling out. But also like I am on my own. So when the good brothers come to stay, looking so much like the enemy, when they come in talking sweetly and meaning it, being loving and meaning it, occupying your thoughts and taking up space, it feels just like that— like an occupation.

Now that I'm grown, my mother speaks more freely about what these men who shaped her youth meant to her. Of my father, she says, looking off into the distance, "He was a ter-rorist." My father controlled our lives through constant sur-veillance and random acts of violence designed to reinforce his control, power, and ownership. But my mother felt like she owed my father loyalty because she felt guilty for "get-ting him shot." And perhaps because she had learned how costly disloyalty could be. Of Bob she says, "He was a fatal attraction" to whom she was attracted, in her words, "because of low self-esteem." Eventually my mother met and married a lovely man, my stepfather, to whom she has been married for more than two decades. Much like these other men, my stepdad, a preacher whom I affectionately call Rev, told me about his own reckoning with the ways his father had been physically abusive toward his mother. "I resolved that I would never put my hands on a woman," Rev told me once. All of these men, my father, my stepfather, and Bob, had to contend with the models handed down to them. But only Rev seemed to come to the right conclusion. My mother, for her part, always felt like her ability to make better romantic choices came from learning to love herself. I'm sure that's part of the story. But it's certainly not all of it.

Self-help gurus, pastors, and poets love to point to Black women's "low self-esteem" as the cause for all Black-girl problems. Just learn to love yourself, we are told. But patriarchy is nothing if not the structurally induced hatred of women. If every woman and girl learned to love herself fiercely, the patriarchy would still be intact; it would demand that she be killed for having the audacity to think she was somebody. Individual blame isn't enough to solve the problem.

How are Black girls supposed to grow up to be Black women in love with themselves in a country built on the structural negation of Black women's humanity and personhood? Too much of the conversation about patriarchy in Black communities pivots on Black women's low self-esteem. Black women are often admonished to make better choices. But my mother left Bob when he didn't treat her right. She almost lost her life for it. The deadliest time for a woman in an abusive relationship is when she decides to leave. Still, despite almost being killed, when things got to be too terrible with my father, she left him, too. From where

I sit, my mama made the right choice to leave every time it became clear that her man wasn't going to treat her right. The abuse had nothing to do with her choices and everything to do with the ways we don't demand that men stop being violent.

Mama says she prayed about when to leave my daddy, asking for the Holy Spirit to show her, a twenty-three-year-old woman, the right time to end things. We should not have to rely on supernatural acts of God to keep women safe. And though my mother is clearly my hero, she deserved better options and more help. Young women encountering violent men today deserve those options, too. It's not enough to teach women how not to attract violent men. We have to spend our time teaching young men how not to be violent men and partners.

Surely Mann and Bob did not hold themselves in high esteem. On the day that my daddy finally, peaceably, retreated from our home, he didn't even look me in the eye. He couldn't. His abdication of responsibility was egregious, yes. But the humiliation of learning that you have taken so much that no one in your home wants anything you have to give is surely an unbearable feeling. The violence that men do demoralizes them, too.

Having a structural analysis of the logics of patriarchy doesn't let Mann and Bob off the hook. War narrows the frame of masculine possibility and tethers it irreparably to violence. In every part of their lives, young men need access to conversations about what it means to be a man in ways that are not rooted in power, dominance, and violence. We owe it to ourselves to imagine what a post-patriarchal Black masculinity might look like. And, frankly, until we have that conversation, men will continue to kill Black women (cis and trans). And they will continue to kill each other.

Perhaps we could start with empathy, though. This is the thing about my father's story that always strikes me—he was a deeply empathetic man, caring greatly about the injustices in the world around him. Social scientists have spoken of a phenomenon that they call the "racial empathy gap," in which people, regardless of race, believe that Black people experience less physical pain than white people experience. This racial empathy gap influences everything from harsher sentences for crime to differential prescribing practices for pain medication based on race.

It strikes me that among Black men and Black women, perhaps there is a gender empathy gap. There is certainly a broader gender empathy gap, in which women are perceived to experience less pain than men and are treated for pain less aggressively than men. Professors Diane Hoffman and Anita Tarzian have found that women frequently receive inadequate treatment for pain, and often that psychological and emotional pain receive less treatment than physical pain. The presence of both a racial empathy gap and a gender empathy gap doesn't bode well for Black women, even though they haven't been a direct focus of these pain-management studies. Because Black women are viewed as preternaturally strong, our pain often goes unnoticed both in the broader world and in our own communities. Black men frequently don't acknowledge our vulnerability, don't seem to think we need defending, and don't feel a political responsibility to hold Black women (who aren't their mothers or sisters or daughters) up and honor them. There seems to be no empathic register for understanding the sheer magnitude of the physical and emotional pain that systems of racism, capitalism, and patriarchy inflict on Black women every day. Black men grow up believing and moving through the world politically as though they have it the toughest, as though their pain matters most, as though Black women cannot possibly be feeling anything similar to the dehumanization and disrespect they have felt. That it might, in many cases, be worse for us seems to many men a preposterous supposition.

My father, for instance, showed far more empathy for the man who shot him than he ever showed for the woman whom he claimed to love the most. Patriarchy numbs men's collective pain sensors, and it causes Black men to not see Black women as worthy of care and concern. To be clear, showing care and concern for the women you want to sleep with or the women who are related to you is not the same as having an overarching commitment to Black women's political, social, and personal well-being as a justice project.

Lest I be mistaken, though, Black men didn't invent patriarchy. Patriarchy is America's daddy issue. America rules the world through war, the same way patriarchs rule families with an iron fist and a Janus-faced promise of either violence or benevolence, depending on which day you catch them, and how well you bow down and do their bidding. Our government does not just wage war abroad. It wages war in Black communities at home, controlling Black folks through surveillance and violence, demanding their submission and compliance. When submission and compliance is not freely offered, the state murders Black men, women, and children, citing the rule of law. The War on Drugs is only the most obvious example of a war that the U.S. government declared and waged on Black communities. That particular war, and the ways it targeted Black men and destroyed Black families, often rendered Black women the spoils of war. And we have been treated as such, as trophies for men to tote around as evidence of their power and greatness. White men who waged war paraded narratives of Black women before the American public in the 1980s, calling them "welfare queens" and "crack addicts" and using hatred of Black women to curry favor with the American public. Black men, demoralized by wars both at home and abroad, took possession of the one thing that was left—the women, treating us as their own kind of trophies, pretty objects that bolstered their social capital while commanding or compelling no responsibility from them for, and to, us.

In his famous 1967 sermon, "Beyond Vietnam," Martin Luther King preached about the "giant triplets of racism, extreme materialism, and militarism." He preached about the "brutal solidarity" that brought together white men and Black men who wouldn't even "live on the same block" back home. King didn't name patriarchy as a founding evil of the U.S. nation-state, but that brutal solidarity that men experienced across race as they went to war cannot be understood outside of a Western patriarchal fantasy that seduces so many brothers whose definition of freedom is a desegregated patriarchy. Black men didn't just experience racial equality on the battlefield; they experienced gender equality, too. After

Truman desegregated the armed forces in time for the Korean Conflict, Black men got to engage in American carnage as equal citizens—not as Black or white, but simply as men. (I'm sure that's how a military brochure might put it.) But what King didn't live long enough to think about was what it would look like for a whole generation of men, Black men in particular, to come back from that war. The Vietnam War was a Pyrrhic victory not only because of its dubious status as a victory abroad, but also because it dropped Black men back off in the same racist hoods they left, this time not only with PTSD, but also with the same limited access to patriarchy and the power of white men that they learned to crave.

So many Black men escaped the racist wars of segregation and criminalization being waged in their own backyards by agreeing to fight America's many racist wars of aggression abroad. That is a perverse model of both masculinity and freedom, and it is Black women and girls who have paid the highest price for it. But Black men have paid the price, too. My daddy was certainly a casualty of war, of the wars Black people wage on each other, when there are no proper outlets for the living out of our dreams or the expression of our rage. Those wars are wars of mundane but devastating violence enacted on those who live in closest proximity to us. It is our own country that uses war as a tool to compel violent submission from those people in other places that we claim to care about. But unchecked violence does not just topple empires. It also devastates men. Both Bob and Mann lost the girl they loved and left a lifetime of resentment, pain, and anger in their wake because they chose to live out the lie that surveillance, control, occupation, and terror are acceptable ways to treat the people they claimed to love, when the truth is that these acts are never acceptable for anyone at all.

BAG LADY

On the very day that Sandra Bland was pulled over in Waller County, Texas, just a stone's throw away from the entrance to her alma mater, Prairie View A&M University, I was on an Amtrak train on a daylong round trip to Harvard University. Bland, a twenty-eight-year-old Chicago resident, was completing a drive to Texas to begin her dream job at Prairie View.

I had been called to come to the Harvard–Smithsonian Center for Astrophysics to speak to young scientists about the importance of employing intersectional perspectives in STEM research. Intersectionality, or the idea that we are all integrally formed and multiply impacted by the different ways that systems of white supremacy, capitalism, and patriarchy affect our lives, was a mostly foreign notion to these young scientists. Intersectional education happens primarily in the kinds of college classrooms that cause conservative politicians to lose their shit on the regular. Intersectionality is considered *fluffy*, *liberal*, *radical*, and certainly not scientific. Intersectionality is not only *not* objective, it sneers at claims to objectivity, arguing that none of us is purely objective. We all come with a perspective and an agenda. We all have investments. We all have skin in the game.

As I stood at the podium doing my thing in that Harvard classroom, no one could tell that my fervent desire was to find somewhere to curl up and weep. I had spent the better part of the four-hour train ride arguing via text message with a high-school sweetheart who had managed to swoop back in with a load of new-school promises that I had recently discovered he had no intention of keeping. On the brink of thirty-five at that point, my career was going exceedingly well, and I thought it the responsible thing to do to begin to turn my attention toward building a family. When I'm not railing at the patriarchy and reconsidering whether a traditional marriage is for me, I spend my time reading romance novels. My favorite romance story plot is always about young lovers who lose touch, reconnect, and then live happily ever after. On this particular summer morning, I was learning for the last time that this would not be my story. I was officially all out of childhood and teenage sweethearts (and there had been a few) with whom to try to make this fantasy work.

About one hour before I arrived, I sent my last curse-filled text to my ex, an equally curse-filled text to my homegirl, who had been offering sympathy, outrage, and possible revenge plots throughout the entire scenario, and then tried to calm my spirit and plaster a smile on my face so I could go explain to this group of eager students the intersectional conundrums that shaped my regular Black-girl life. I couldn't fall apart like I wanted to because, well, I'm a Black girl, and we don't get the luxury of doing frivolous shit like that. This was an invitation to speak at Harvard, after all. Business always comes first, broken hearts later. Black women's historian Darlene Clark Hine coined a term for the performance I was putting on. She called it the "culture of dissemblance," this enigmatic way that Black women in the late-nineteenth and early-twentieth centuries moved through the world, often doing race work of the type I was doing that day, giving the appearance of being open while fully obscuring the operations of their inner lives from public view.

While I was busy dissembling, Sandra Bland was in another part of the world completing what amounts to a return migration back to the South from Chicago, the very city that two generations earlier had seen so many Black people fleeing North to escape the pervasive, quotidian horror of Southern state-sanctioned racial violence. She was just a few hundred yards from completing her journey when she ran into a twenty-first century specter of a violence that we all hoped was long gone. When she made it to University Drive, the street that runs into the campus of Prairie View, a Waller County police officer began following her. She thought he wanted to pass, so she pulled over. He pulled over behind her, and was apparently planning to write her a citation for "failure to signal a lane change." She could almost see the university from where she was sitting. She was that close to her dream job.

Instead, officer Brian Encinia decided to harass, assault, and arrest Bland because she refused to be servile during the traffic stop. She did not berate the officer but she did let him know she wasn't pleased that he had pulled her over on a bullshit charge. Incensed by her lack of deference and her seeming lack of fear, Encinia grabbed his Taser, opened the door, reached into the vehicle, and yanked Sandra Bland out of her car, while yelling at her, "I will light you up." A local bystander stopped to tape the incident, and Bland, who was a great supporter of the Black Lives Matter movement, thanked the bystander for taping. She narrated that the officer had just slammed her head into the ground and cuffed her wrists so tightly, she thought they might break. A Black woman officer can be heard off-camera telling a struggling Bland, "Well, you shoulda thought about that."

Bland spent the weekend trying to arrange for someone to bring the $500 needed to bail her out of jail. Five hundred dollars is such a small amount, but the cost is prohibitively high in a world where Black women between the ages of eighteen and sixty-four have been estimated to have only about $100 of net wealth. Not only do most Black women not have $500 to spare in case of emergencies, but many don't have networks of family or friends with that kind of money to spare either.

On Monday morning, July thirteenth, at around 9:00 A.M., Sandra Bland was found dead. The official narrative is that she hanged herself by placing a trash bag around her neck. I don't know what happened to Bland in that jail cell. It's easier to believe—and entirely plausible—that rogue police officers murdered her. In March 2016, Brian Encinia was fired and charged with misdemeanor perjury for giving a false account of what happened at the traffic stop. In June 2017, local prosecutors dropped all charges; Encinia surrendered his law enforcement license and agreed that he would never work in law enforcement again.

Caring for Black women's actual lives means sitting with the acuteness of our fragility. We break, too. Police at the White House killed Miriam Carey in 2013. She was a mother suffering from severe postpartum depression, who, it seems, took a wrong turn at the White House gates with her baby daughter strapped into the backseat. She was killed in a hail of bullets while her baby daughter sat helpless. Tanisha Anderson of Cleveland, Ohio, experienced a mental health crisis, which caused her children to contact police for help to assist their mother in taking her medicine. Instead an officer handcuffed her, and when she began to struggle, he restrained her by putting a knee in her back, effectively smothering her while her children watched. The county medical examiner ruled her death a homicide, and the police department settled with the family for over two million dollars. The system's response to seeing us bend is to break us entirely.

For Black girls, many of us teeter on that brink. If one more thing goes wrong, we feel like we just can't make it. We go to church like Bland, a church girl herself. There, preachers tell us, "Your blessing is just around the bend. Keep pressing." On March 1, 2015, Bland uploaded a video to her vlog *Sandy Speaks*. She admitted to struggling with depression and PTSD, and spoke out against the stigma and shame that many who struggle with depression feel. She apologized for not having vlogged regularly, and told her listeners, "I'm just a human." And then she mentioned that though she had missed church that morning, she watched a bit of the service, and the morning's message had been about faith.

Just four months later, that same faith caused Bland to press her way to Texas for her dream job. Through *Sandy Speaks*, Bland talked about everything from her recent struggles with depression after losing a pregnancy to her outrage over the police killings of unarmed Black people and her support for the Black Lives Matter Movement. Unlike the race women of old, Sandy Bland did not dissemble. She shared her private struggles right alongside her political views.

On the morning of July 10, 2015, Sandra Bland and I were two Black women chasing our dreams, even in the aftermath of our heartbreak. I know exactly what it feels like to pack all of my belongings into the car and drive more than a thousand miles to the gates of a university that holds my career hopes and dreams. I've done it more than once. And I know how much I relied on my faith in God and myself to travel every mile.

It's classic for writers to spend time waxing eloquent about the possibilities and perils of life's metaphoric journeys, and the roads we either do or don't travel. But the dangers that attend Black people's actual travels are not in any guise metaphoric. Reminiscent of earlier periods of racial terror for African Americans, traffic stops have again become the pretext for the reckless taking of Black life by police. In April 2015, South Carolina police officer Michael Slager killed Walter Scott after stopping him for a broken taillight. Slager was charged with murder and brought to trial. Though a local barber who was walking through the area shot clear video of Slager shooting an unarmed Scott as he was running away, a judge declared a mistrial in December 2016 after a local jury failed to return a verdict. In May 2017, Slager pled guilty to federal charges that he violated Scott's civil rights. He is now serving time in federal prison. In August 2016, after Korryn Gaines, a twenty-three-year-old mother from Baltimore, fail-ed to pay a traffic citation, members of the police force arrived at her house to serve her a warrant for failure to appear in court. The standoff ended when police kicked in Gaines's door, shot and killed her, and shot her five-year-old son. And in July 2016, a Minnesota police officer shot and killed Phi-lando Castile, after Castile requested permission to pull out his gun and concealed-weapons permit for the officer's inspection during a traffic stop for a broken taillight. The officer was acquitted of all charges, despite damning dash cam video suggesting that Castile did nothing wrong.

Because traffic stops are frequently a life-or-death matter for Black people, stopping traffic has become one of the primary modes of protest for the Black Lives Matter movement (BLM). The shutdown of major interstate highways began in August 2014, after a police officer shot eighteen-year-old Michael Brown and left his dead body lying in the street for four and a half hours. In the weeks that followed, across the country from St. Louis to Atlanta to Oakland, protestors began to form human barriers across major highways while holding signs and chanting, "Black Lives Matter," and "Hands Up, Don't Shoot."

Charlene Carruthers, national director of the Black Youth

Project 100, has said "When people disrupt highways and streets, it is about disrupting business as usual. It's also about giving a visual that folks are willing to put their bodies on the line to create the kind of world we want to live in." Feminist activist Naomi Wolf once said, "For a protest to be effective, you have to stop traffic." Carruthers understands the stakes of Black people putting their bodies on the line to stop traffic as a kind of visual prophecy of the world we want to see, a world where we all can go to our destinations safely and soundly or no one can. When they put their bodies on the line, they dramatize the danger for all people who are stuck in traffic.

Black women have long been aware of what it means to be stuck in traffic, confined to the intersections of social discourses that bypass us on their way to futures to which we don't have access. In the late 1980s, legal scholar Kimberlé Crenshaw named this seemingly shared quality of Black women's lives *intersectionality*. Intersectionality makes clear the ways that systems of power interact in Black women's lives to restrict social mobility and to hinder us from moving unencumbered through the social sphere. Pulled over at a traffic stop, peering intently down University Drive to the destiny she had created for herself, Sandra Bland was yanked into a future that precisely mirrored the violent Black past that we are presently—and collectively—obsessed with escaping. She was right there. Right there. At the intersection of destiny, dreams, and death. Death won, assisted in its victory by those with real power.

Five months before she was killed by police, Korryn Gaines was pulled over in Baltimore County for a traffic stop.

She had replaced the front license plate on her car with a cardboard sign that read "free traveler." The back plates had a similar cardboard sign that read, "Any government official who compromises this pursuit to happiness and right to travel will be held criminally responsible and fined, as this is a natural right and freedom." I know to "regular," "law-abiding" folks, Korryn sounds crazy. Hers is a kind of brazenness the world tries to beat out of Black girls before they reach adulthood. For many who are apologists for state violence, her declaration of her freedom and her rights sounded like an invitation to harassment. But let's do this young Black woman, one who had undoubtedly heard of Sandra Bland's story, the courtesy of suspending our disbelief. She chose to be eccentric, defiant, *outrageous*, and, dare I say, visionary in a world where Black women and girls don't often get to do any of these things without lethal consequences.

There is a thin line between clarity and craziness, and sometimes clarity can be crazy-making. For there is a profound argument in the particular terms through which Korryn Gaines chose to elaborate her freedom project. She argued, by way of a makeshift license plate, that the pursuit of happiness and the right to travel are natural rights, rights that are endemic to any declaration of freedom. The struggle by Black people to obtain the free and full exercise of their natural rights and continual forms of structural opposition to these rights have been a fundamental feature of what it means to be Black in America. To get bogged down or distracted by the policy and procedure elements of her approach is to miss the soundness of her conclusions. By declaring her rights to travel, to freedom, and to happiness to be natural rights, Korryn Gaines invoked a very particular political discourse about the origin of our natural rights. If freedom to travel and freedom to be happy are civil rights or legal rights, they exist entirely at the whim and fancy of the U.S. government. If however, these matters are natural rights, they are not bound by the exigencies of policy and procedure. The problem is not that Korryn Gaines believed these ideas about herself, but rather that she chose to make them explicit.

How can this Black woman's notions of freedom, her audacity in trying to live free, seem so preposterous and exasperating and so utterly reasonable and exhilarating at the same time? More than any of us, she seemed to have a clear vision of what freedom for Black women looked like—the ability to get in a vehicle of your choosing, strap your babies safely into the backseat, and make your way to the place where you were trying to go. This conception of freedom, the ability to travel unencumbered to the places where you need to go, is something Black women have been fighting for since they first encountered America. I think of twenty-one-year-old Ida B. Wells who, in 1883, was violently removed from the ladies' car of a train in Memphis, Tennessee, because "colored women" were not allowed to sit there. Because segregation laws were not yet cemented, Wells tried to flout the unspoken mandate to segregate, so that she could read her newspaper in the much nicer ladies' car in peace. Instead, the conductor and two other passengers tried to drag her to her "place" in the colored car. She chose to get off the train instead.

This long history of Black women enduring violent harass-

ment while they are on their way somewhere—anywhere—
makes Korryn Gaines's demands to be recognized and
respected as a "free traveler" far less preposterous. I'm also
struck by the intimacy of these encounters, the moment
when, as Bland and Wells experienced, suddenly a white
man is putting his hands on you, yanking you violently away
from your intended journey. I wonder about what Ida Wells
might have been reading, about what Sandy Bland and
Korryn Gaines might have been bumping on the radio,
about what thoughts might have streamed through their
consciousness as they were on their way somewhere, anywhere. At twenty-one, Wells had her fair share of young men
jockeying for her affections. I wonder if her thoughts moved
somewhere between her love life, her love of pretty dresses,
and the injustices she was undoubtedly reading about in
the paper.

The tragic consequences of these traffic and train encounters make clear that intersectionality has intimate consequences. What does it look like for Black women to move
freely through space when we are always confronting the
precariousness of life at the intersections of race and gender,
of class and mental health, of love and dreams? Erykah Badu
once famously cautioned Black women about the costs of
carrying around too much baggage: "Bag lady, you gone
miss yo' bus. You can't hurry up cause you got too much
stuff." Badu then coolly advises, "Pack light." But, of course,
that is not entirely our choice.

Black women did not agree to or apply for the job of baggage handlers for the nation. With histories as forced labor-
ers and forced breeders, so much of our employment history

in this country has simply not been up to us. Our lives are strewn about with structurally deposited baggage. If we assume the radical position that it isn't ours to carry, we are called lazy. Degenerate. Angry. Irresponsible. The nation waves its fingers at us in accusation, demanding that we take the weight. And, often, we accede to these demands, taking the weight against our will, but taking it nonetheless. Black women take it upon ourselves to challenge stereotypes, to raise respectable children, to build homes, communities, and churches despite our chronic condition of underemployment. We are masters of wresting sustenance from insufficiency. We combat structurally imposed trauma much as Erykah Badu demanded of both herself and us—by taking responsibility for the weight we carry.

I don't even have to go all the way back to Ida B. Wells in the 1880s to be appalled by the amount of social and structural baggage foisted upon the backs of Black women. The 1980s was hell on the social image of Black women, who were vilified and demonized as money-grubbing welfare queens and drug-abusing crack fiends birthing crack babies that the system couldn't handle. Oprah Winfrey as Miss Sofia in Steven Spielberg's 1985 screen adaptation of Alice Walker's *The Color Purple* uttered one of the most memorable and damning lines about the terrible burdens that America (and Black men) had heaped upon Black women. "All my life, I had to fight," she told Celie after her husband Harpo tried to beat her in an assertion of male dominance. There's a reason why Black women my age can recite lines from *The Color Purple* at will. The film is iconic because it dared, following Alice Walker's lead, to suggest to America that Black women were the heroes and not the villains of the American national story. It dared to suggest to a watching world that the baggage we carry is not of our own stitching. And while we Black girls always recite these lines to each other in a humorous context, it is mostly humorous because just underneath the surface, the truth of what we say in jest leaps at us with the clarity of an Alvin Ailey performance. If you hear one sister saying to another, "Don't do it, Miss Celie," you better move out the way, 'cause somebody is liable to get cut.

Black women powerbrokers of the 1990s undertook a full-scale rescue mission to resuscitate the culturally devastated image of Black womanhood handed to us in the 1980s. In the 1990s, during my tween and adolescent years, I watched women my mother's age explode the Black women's chick lit and self-help industries. Books by Iyanla Vanzant and Susan L. Taylor were a staple in my household. Together with books by (and about) Oprah, Maya Angelou, Terry Mc-Millan, the telltale pink *Women's Devotional Bible* (with which every Black girl of a certain age is familiar), and copies of *Essence* and *Ebony* magazines, I watched my mama fashion a clearly Black-woman, girl-centered household for the two of us. These books and magazines acted as therapy for my working-class single mom who couldn't afford to sit on someone's sofa once a week to discuss her problems. She had a daughter to feed and bills to pay. This bookshelf and coffee-table therapy gave birth to two unspoken mantras that shaped our life together: "Take care of business" and "Daughter, heal thyself."

My mother used the explosion of a body of literature that spoke to Black women's interior lives to get hers together.

After the abuse she suffered during my childhood, my mother, tired of being used and abused, began the process of healing herself in my tween and teen years. Years later, she would tell me, "I wanted better for you, and if I wanted better for you, then I had to want better for myself." I watched my mom read Iyanla's *Yesterday, I Cried* and *In the Meantime*. And I watched as she intently listened, when a rare day off permitted her to, to Iyanla on *The Oprah Winfrey Show*. I was a keen observer of my mother, and I knew she connected to this material even though I did not always understand why. I liked to read *Essence* and *Ebony* but didn't much care for the rest of it. I saw my mother's admiration for Susan Taylor's monthly "In the Spirit" column. I read it and thought it sounded good, but too heavy and fluffy for my Black-girl tastes. My mother was a woman, as Alice Walker once said of her character Meridian, "in the process of changing her mind." I watched my mother change her mind about her worth and value and then reflect that shift in her romantic choices. She freed herself from a cycle of abuse and, in so doing, saved her own life.

I believe wholeheartedly in the internal spiritual work that Black women must do to save our own lives. But I also wonder whether our spiritual work is a match for the structural systems that would crush us alive. Audre Lorde famously said, "If I didn't define myself for myself, I would be crunched into other people's fantasies for me and eaten alive." But what do we do with this push for self-definition and self-recognition in a system that would crush us anyway? It crushed Sandra Bland. It crushed Korryn Gaines. It has crushed untold numbers of trans Black women, who have been killed simply for having the audacity to live their truth.

My own mother modeled the importance of taking care of one's spirit as a means of saving oneself. This was the model of Black womanhood that shaped my coming-of-age, and it still shapes how I move through the world as a grown woman. In the Oprah-Iyanla-Susan era, my mother would always say to me, when I came home crying about being bullied by mean girls at school, "The only behavior you can change is your own. What behavior can you change so you can avoid this kind of attention?" Even if in the end the "behavior" I changed was my own mind-set, such that the taunts didn't bother me as much, the point was that my mother believed in my moving through the world with a spirit of self-possession. She raised me to be a Black girl who believes (sometimes stridently) in her own mind and her own counsel. Akin to that, I believe that each of us is responsible for doing our own emotional work. We can't hope to have healthy relationships of any type if we are unwilling to own our shit.

I am struck by the manner in which my mother's ability to show up to and heal her own life was made possible in the particular world of the 1990s, a brief moment where Black women were allowed to see themselves and their full set of possibilities. The last decade of the twentieth century found the nation discovering for the first time what Black business owners and corporations had long known—that Black women were a target demographic for cosmetics, self-help literature, and chick lit. In 1991, Maybelline launched its "Shades of You" campaign, becoming the first mainstream cosmetics

line to explicitly focus on women of color. Consumer culture scholar and professor Robert Weems has marked this
as a "watershed" event, which led to a proliferation of more
than a dozen Black women–focused cosmetic lines in a two-
year period. Today, I have my pick of cosmetic products that
can match and complement my dark brown skin tone, but
in my adolescent years, such products were just coming into
existence. Weems suggests that so much of Black people's
experience of citizenship has been tied to consumerism; so
when Black women became a mainstream target demographic in the 1990s, they experienced new levels of cultural visibility that expanded to other arenas like books and
movies.

Terry McMillan reached blockbuster success with her
1992 novel *Waiting to Exhale*. My mother and I then hustled to the public library on a Saturday morning to pick up
her earlier novels *Mama* and *Disappearing Acts*. Or rather,
she picked up Terry McMillan novels, and I checked out
Mildred Taylor books like *Roll of Thunder, Hear My Cry* and
Let the Circle Be Unbroken. Oprah officially reigned as
the queen of daytime television, providing a platform for
Iyanla Vanzant to dig into the inner lives of struggling Black
women and call forth a healing. And Susan Taylor's over-
sight of *Essence* magazine with both her "In the Spirit" column and her mind/body/spirit approach to presenting Black
women's issues created a felicitous set of social conditions
for Black women to come to voice in ways that were more
personal than political.

Suddenly, Black women professionals were talking about
the personal stakes of being Black women in a world that

didn't love us. Oprah and Iyanla, for instance, talked little about racism, sexism, and poverty. But they spoke a lot about the terrible choices we make when we have low self-esteem and don't love ourselves. I wonder if Sandra Bland watched episodes of *Iyanla, Fix My Life* as she struggled to overcome her depression. Now that I'm grown, I regularly pick up *O, The Oprah Magazine*, looking for tips to fix my own life. As a twentysomething, I ran across a column on narcissism in *O* magazine, and that column named for me the emotional abuse I endured for so many years from an old boyfriend. Reading those words helped me to stop hoping that he would ever change, because narcissists never do. Those words gave me the language to free myself from that relationship, to know that I deserved better.

I struggle, then, with how to simultaneously hold the competing truths that shape Black women's public and private lives. On the one hand, I have made many a bad decision, tolerating bad friends and even worse dudes, because I didn't love myself as well as I should have. Therefore, I merely accepted what others offered, even when it was so much less than what I am worth. That is the truth. And my process of learning that truth was deeply personal and has been deeply transformative.

On the other hand, individual transformation is neither a substitute for nor a harbinger of structural transformation. Holding oneself in perpetually low esteem is a structurally induced condition. Patriarchy propagates a whole series of narratives about Black women that are designed to make us hate ourselves. Melissa Harris-Perry argues that Black women carry a great amount of shame because of our inability to fully inhabit the American dream. In 1965, when Senator Daniel Patrick Moynihan argued that Black communities were caught in a tangle of pathology because our communities had a disproportionate number of female-led households, his conclusions had both affective and social dimensions. His 1965 report, "The Negro Family: The Case for National Action," offered social and political recommendations focused on ways to help Black men become breadwinners again so they could assume their "rightful" place at the head of Black families. But the affective goal of his infamous *Moynihan Report* was to shame Black women for the very mundane magic involved in our making a way out of no way.

That shame persists well into the twenty-first century, when more than 70 percent of Black households are female-led. Black women have proportionally higher rates of abortion than any other group. There is no shame in having an abortion. I consider the right to choose the conditions under which one becomes a parent to be one of the most important social values. But I believe that decades of discourse about poor Black women and unwed Black mothers being "welfare queens" who unfairly take more from the system than they put in has shamed many Black women into not bearing children that they otherwise might consider having. The idea that only middle-class, straight, married women deserve to start families is both racist and patriarchal.

The fact that our society honestly believes that poor women don't have the right to start families because they may require public assistance obscures the variety of ways that middle-class families do receive public assistance. White families have been the primary beneficiaries of both public and corporate welfare in the form of redlining policies that drove down property values in Black neighborhoods, making those neighborhoods undesirable for businesses, families, and schools. They have been beneficiaries of favorable bank-loan terms to help them purchase safe, affordable, quality housing. They are the beneficiaries of marital and housing tax breaks and the disproportionate beneficiaries of the dwindling number of quality public schools that we have left.

Public discourse on the right paints a picture of brazen Black and Brown teenagers and unmarried mothers having baby after baby that they can't support to game the system. In fact, the discourse about Korryn Gaines after she was killed was that she was a bad Black mother who used her son as a human shield against the cops. But she told her five-year-old to document what was happening to her, teaching him how to train her smartphone's video camera on her as she talked. Less outrage was reserved for the police who decided that shooting her son who, thankfully, survived was a reasonable price to pay for apprehending his mother, who had committed the crime of failing to pay a traffic ticket. When I talk to Black women in my community, many of them feel shame and guilt about not being respectable Black women in traditional two-parent homes.

In middle school, there were only two Black girls in my school's gifted and talented program, my friend Holly and me. We took to each other quickly because Black girls find each other as a means to survive. We were both working-class girls raised by single moms. I insisted on being a good girl, while Holly was definitely a rebel. By her junior and my senior year of high school, Holly was pregnant. Neither of us were strangers to teen pregnancy in our community. Black girls in my community had been getting pregnant since I was in the sixth grade.

So when Holly got pregnant, I was concerned and a little sad, but not surprised. She fit the cautionary tale that I was steadfastly trying to avoid, because I am the daughter of a teen mom. After many years we lost contact and reconnected via Facebook. By then, she had had five children and was on her way to baby number six.

One day, we inboxed just to catch up and she told me of the multiple degrees in nursing she had secured and how proud she was of her family. I was proud of her and also feeling just a bit lonely. Yes, Holly's path to family was risky, but she had made it. And I had toed the line and followed the rules, a little too well, perhaps. Now I find myself in my thirties with few prospects of having children in a traditional two-parent family. In fact, my late thirties are beset with the heaviness of receding childbearing options. Still, Holly said to me in the inbox, "I'm trying. I don't want to be another statistic." The irony is that I traded being one kind of Black woman statistic for another. I'm now among the scores of professional Black women who are unmarried. This, too, is seen as a failure—as just more evidence of the pervasive social undesirability of Black women.

With her six children by multiple fathers and her multiple nursing degrees to boot, Holly challenged every stereotype I might have been invested in believing. And when my doctor, at my behest, began to walk me through the process and the cost of retrieving and freezing my eggs, I began to wonder if maybe I had done something wrong. Many Black women like me are so obsessed with the idea of not having babies too early that frequently it ends up being too late. No statistic can adequately capture Holly's story; she didn't let respectability politics have the last word.

Black women pay the highest costs for investing in respectability politics. First, it breeds distrust between middle-class striving women and poor women of color. We (middle-class women) are taught that those women, who were once "fast-tailed girls" make us all look bad. I never thought about poor women as making me look bad, because my community of women was working-class. And my mother often reminded me when I became a bit too frivolous with her money: "Child, we are poor." Like many, many Americans and most Black folks I know, we lived paycheck to paycheck. And given the dubious origins of my birth, my family certainly wouldn't have been invited to Jack and Jill. But I knew very early on that I didn't want to be like the girls in my middle school, saddled with children I couldn't support and doomed to a lifetime of low-wage work with little opportunity for advancement.

These are the narratives that working-class "good" girls buy into in order to make our way out of the hood. The goal to "not be like them" animates our drive and our hustle. But now that I'm grown, I no longer believe that Black women should imbibe shame and blame for all the creative ways that we build families and lives, arrange fulfilling partnerships, and work to maintain safe homes and steady employment.

I spent my twenties and most of my thirties waiting on a partner to show up before I would ever consider children, because I never wanted to be a single mother. I bought into the idea that making good choices around education and career would entitle me to a broader set of options in every part of my life. But the world doesn't work that way for Black women. In my college, the female-to-male ratio was 3 to 2. Even assuming that everyone had hooked up in heterosexual pairings, one-third of Black girls were automatically going to be assed out. When I graduated from Howard without having even one boyfriend there, it didn't dawn on me that I was one of the 33 percent. The optimism of my twenties would not let me consider that these numbers would not improve over the course of my life. My friends and I didn't realize the structural clusterfuck that shaped Black partnering options until we were already in the thick of things. I'll say more about all that in the chapter titled "Love in a Hopeless Place." But suffice it to say that we thought, as all young people do, that we had endless time, that our chosen boos would arrive, and that our advanced degrees would bring us into a world of men with advanced degrees and earning potential, too. It hasn't worked out that way for a great many of us.

In my thirties I became an unwilling member of the Sisterhood of Fibroid Havers. Black women disproportionately struggle with fibroid tumors, and the medical science continues to offer little explanation. After my fibroid surgery, a successful outpatient procedure that I thought would buy me a little more time, my doctor, a lovely Black woman gynecologist, told me, "More than likely, your fibroids will return. You have a uterus that makes fibroids." Perhaps the saddest part of being reminded of the dreaded biological clock was having to tell my mother that, since I had no partner in sight, I might not be able to give her grandchildren. For the first time, I began to wonder whether I should have been less regimented and more reckless in my twenties, when I was younger and had eggs to spare. Black women deserve more options than these extremes—that the same choices we make to not ruin our lives as young people become the choices that make us miserable twenty years later.

Part of what friendship has meant in my thirties is supporting my homegirls in their thirties and forties who have limited partnering options, and even fewer options for starting families. The intimate consequences of all these good-ass choices we have made are relentlessly brutal. Yes, folks are quick to say: Adopt. Freeze your eggs. Try in vitro. But with what money? Black women in prime child-rearing age have negligible net wealth. Many of these single women, as first-generation middle-class with loads of educational debt and without a two-income household, have no way to fund a creative family structure. The weight of the absence—of the partners who didn't show up, of the children you didn't get to have, of the uterus robbed by fibroids—is a burden none of us was properly prepared to bear.

How much of this baggage can we reasonably be expected to carry? On that July morning that I found myself at Harvard, I walked off the train carrying more baggage than I walked onto it with. Life (and, more to the point, bullshit like heartbreaks and racism and sexism) bequeaths to us baggage. The end of that relationship was my last shot at a serious relationship before I reached advanced maternal age. He couldn't appreciate the urgent consequences of what was clearly routine fuckery for him. At any point, he could turn things around and have a child. I could not. That's how male privilege is set up.

This is why songs like "Bag Lady," which point out this baggage to us and act like we are holding all of it of our own accord, are summarily unhelpful. The unfair part is that folks are far more concerned with policing how Black women carry the baggage than with reducing the load hoisted upon us in the first place. When I read fluffy self-help literature or attend church services where usually male preachers tell usually female parishioners that our social conditions are largely a result of our personal failings and individual bad choices, I often want to throw the book or walk out of the service. But while I have, in fact, walked out of service, I have, thus far, refrained from throwing books. Those who preach this sermon, whether in print or from the pulpit, think they are "empowering" Black women to address the conditions we face.

But "empowerment" is a tricky word. It's also a decidedly neoliberal word that places the responsibility for combating systems on individuals. Neoliberalism is endlessly concerned with "personal responsibility" and individual self-regulation. It tells us that in a free market, devoid of any regulation or accountability at the top, what happens to those on the bottom is entirely our fault. Did we have enough drive? Enough vision? Enough hustle to change our condition? The politics of personal empowerment suggests to us that if we simply "free our minds, then our asses will follow." I'm not convinced that this is true. Why? Have you ever noticed that people who have real "power"—wealth, job security, influence—don't attend "empowerment" seminars? Power is not attained from books and seminars. Not alone, anyway. Power is conferred by social systems. Empowerment and power are not the same thing. We must quit mistaking the two. Better yet, we must quit settling for one when what we really need is the other.

Those who feel "empowered" talk about their personal power to change their individual condition. Those with actual power make decisions that are of social and material consequence to themselves and others. Sandra Bland used her faith to empower her to cope with her depression and pursue her dreams; she met the limits of her narratives of faith and empowerment on the shoulder of University Drive, and subsequently in a Waller County jail cell. Empowerment looks like cultivating the wisdom to make the best choices we can out of what are customarily a piss-poor set of options. Power looks like the ability to create better options. The powerlessness and capriciousness of being repeatedly jammed up at the personal and political crossroads of one's intersections while a watching world pretends not to see you there, needing help, is how it feels to be a Black woman on an ordinary day.

Individual solutions to collective problems cannot work, no matter how personally empowering they may feel. I could have been Sandra Bland, because I have certainly "mouthed off" to an officer on more than one occasion. I could have been Holly, but for a few different choices and opportunities. And I am my mother's child, a daughter who believes wholeheartedly that my first patient is always me. I refuse, however, to be America's bag lady, resigned to hauling around a load of cultural refuse heaped on me by the nation.

First our country tried to rob us of seats on the bus. One generation of our foremothers, women like Claudette Colvin, Rosa Parks, and Pauli Murray, fought for us to have a seat of our own choosing. Now our generation struggles even to catch the bus, weighed down as we are by the lies about our worth, our dignity, and our worthiness. Claudette Colvin was an unwed pregnant teen when she was arrested for refusing to give up her seat on a bus in 1955. Rosa Parks was a married, respectable officer of the NAACP when she was arrested for refusing to give up her seat. Pauli Murray was a masculine-performing queer Black woman when she was arrested for refusing to give up her seat. Every kind of Black woman has a stake in the proverbial "bus."

Every kind of Black woman has fought for our right to be free to travel in pursuit of dreams and destiny. One way to start shedding the baggage is to start telling our truths, to start opening the bags and exposing the lies that weigh us down. The weight of the nation is not ours to carry.

GROWN-WOMAN THEOLOGY

The summer before I left home for graduate school, I drove down to the rural Louisiana countryside to sit on the porch with my grandma. As I took the four steps up to the house, face scowling at the hot Louisiana sun beating down on my brow, my Gram squinted at me, called me by my nickname, and declared, "It's time for you to start having sex!"

I'm sure my eyes bugged out of my head, as the horror dawned upon me that this wasn't going to be any old regular visit to the country. There was an accusation in her words, as though this was something my twenty-two-year-old self should have been doing forever. For the record, I had in fact had a bit of sex by age twenty-two; for my twenty-second birthday my homegirl, horrified at my post-college near-virginal status, took me to a sex shop and purchased a vibrator for me. There was a classic Black woman *read* in my grandmother's words, an unspoken "If that's true, *I can't tell*." Of course she couldn't! I was steeped in all kinds of Christian guilt about the little bit of sex that I had had and the copious amounts of vibrating I had done. That, coupled with the asshole I had chosen for a first partner, meant that I wasn't having particularly joyful or enthusiastic sex, and most times I was in sanctified denial about my desire to be sexual in the first place.

I made it onto the porch and sat down to listen to my good Christian seventy-five-year-old grandmother, a lady given to elaborate hats and bejeweled suits on the Sundays she didn't usher at church, extol the virtues of sex to unmarried me. "Back in my day, we did it," she said. I squirmed. *Who ever wants to know this about their grandma?* "Don't ever let anybody tell you we didn't. We went up in the woods and did it, but we did it." By the time I was born, Grandmama had been a widow for ten years. She and my grandfather got married and then had their children. In the way that none of us is ever inclined to think about the sex lives of our grandparents, it never even occurred to me to ask about whether my grandmother had waited until marriage to have sex or to consider the sexual practices of young Black folks in the 1940s.

Comically, she explained to me that I should have sex, but only if my partner was willing to wear "one of those combos." *What the hell is a combo?* I wondered. *Condoms.* Her colorful descriptions and gestures made it clear that she meant "condoms!" Grandmama had not been able to hear well since her teen years, when some kind of fever damaged her ears. So, when someone said "condom," she heard "combos." When I heard combos, I thought of the hilarious conversations I had had years earlier with my high-school boyfriend about exactly what *combos* of birth control we would use so I wouldn't ruin all my overachieving Black-girl life goals, if I ever gave in and gave him some. For my Gram, access to birth control mattered greatly. She told me that she would have opted for only two children rather than the six she'd had (and raised and loved) if birth control had been widely available to Black women in the 1950s and 1960s in rural Louisiana. "But we couldn't get the stuff," she told me. In her own way, I think my grandmama let me know that the women's movement was a win for Black women, too, because in the twenty-first century, it meant her grand-daughter could have a wonderful sex life without bearing children, until she chose to.

My grandmother had already developed a pragmatic blend of both feminism and Christianity that worked in the context of her life, as a poor rural Southern Black woman born two years before the Great Depression. I was still far too much of a Christian zealot to be either pragmatic or femi-nist. My grandmother didn't have all the language for these differing ideological positions, but she had good sense. She looked at me with those laser eyes that Black mamas use to see right through you, and commanded me to "start having sex." She meant real, good sex. Sex that left you with telltale signs that you had been touched right and handled with care. I didn't exude sexuality. I didn't exude grown woman-hood. I did not look like a Black girl comfortable in my own skin. Because I wasn't.

I was trapped in a raging battle between my spirit and my flesh. The evangelical teachings of the Baptist churches in which I grew up insisted that our flesh—our bodies and their

longings and impulses—were sinful, dangerous, and unhealthy. We were admonished each week to bring our unruly
flesh in submission to our "spirit man." Having heard this
every Sunday of my life I did not understand how my grandmother, our beloved family matriarch, could dare advocate
that I let my flesh win. Clearly, I wasn't ready for the grown-
woman theology that this holy woman offered to me that
day. Frankly, I thought she had gotten ahold of some terrible
theology, and I was determined to live my life as a good
evangelical should. I had life goals and desires for success
that my provincial grandmother, who once told me to go to
the local college and then "get a good clerical job," clearly did
not understand. Sex messed with your head, boys were fun,
but trouble, and a baby before you wanted one, could ruin
your life. This was my credo in triplicate.

Dismissing grandmother's words was easy. I felt that my
theology, informed indirectly by the advent of the "True
Love Waits" purity campaigns of the 1990s, and my ability
to recite by rote all the Bible verses condemning sex before
marriage made my spiritual perspective more sophisticated,
more informed, more correct. I had imbibed a set of social
ideas about Black girlhood and womanhood rooted in the
fear of being a failure and the social shame of becoming a
statistic. I nearly worshipped my mother, but I didn't want to
be a teen mother as she had been. I wanted to finish college,
something my birth had prevented her from doing. By the
time grandmother sat me down for *the talk*, I was twenty-
two, had completed two college degrees, and was on my
way to a Ph.D. program. By local standards, I had already
made it.

In 1993, the year that I turned thirteen, Lifeway Bookstores, the publishing arm of the Southern Baptist Convention, made their intervention in the "sex sells" culture wars with their True Love Waits sexual abstinence campaign. Christians wanted to talk about sex, too, even if only to suggest that no one should be having it. That is, unless they were of age, straight, married, and preferably Christian. For clarification, even though I was Southern and Baptist, my church and most Black churches in the South were not in fact part of the Southern Baptist Convention (SBC). Those were the white Baptists—the ones who were pro-slavery and pro-segregation. In fact, the SBC did not issue a formal apology for slavery until 1995.

The purity discourse that emerged from Southern white evangelicalism is not separable from the racialized discourse of sexuality and purity that these same Christians have shaped for the whole of American history. The regulation of sexuality by white Christians in the United States has always been about the propagation of a socially acceptable and pristine nuclear family worthy of having the American dream, a family that was heterosexual, middle class, and white. Because my social circles were mostly white, I had a front-row seat to the incursion of True Love Waits programs among my white classmates.

Peppered among their discussions about youth mission trips to Mexico were conversations about promise rings, purity pledges, and True Love Waits classes. My church had a makeshift youth group that met irregularly and a teen Sunday School class, which I attended faithfully. There was no purity talk beyond bringing the flesh into submission. There were no mission trips or classes devoted to sex ed. What my community also had was a teen pregnancy problem—it was not uncommon for Black girls to get pregnant in my middle school or my high school. I can remember only one white teen mom in high school (although I am sure there were a few others), and absolutely none in middle school. For me, the equation was simple. In communities where they talked about sexual abstinence and "waiting," they didn't have a teen pregnancy problem. In my community, where no such conversations were had, teen pregnancy was rampant.

These messages about success, whiteness, abstinence, and Christianity converged for me. Black kids accused me of acting white, but the white kids I knew loved Jesus (like I did), did well in school (like me), and got to have interesting discussions and experiences at church (which I didn't). I have already mentioned the particular challenges of growing up a nerdy Black girl in a predominantly white school system. One way that I internalized white supremacy in my honors classes, which were 95 percent white and in which the kids were overwhelmingly Christian, was to associate the success I sought with the kind of whiteness and morality that shaped my classmates' lives. White privilege works by making the advantages white people have invisible while making the supposedly "poor" choices of people of color hypervisible. For instance, on the surface, it simply looks like white people have better access to education, jobs, and housing because they make better choices or because they work harder. And, conversely, it looks like Black people have less access to these same things because they are lazy. In fact, in most opinion polls, white people believe that Black people don't work as hard as they do. And what is perhaps most interesting is that white people believe this myth as much today as they believed it in the racially volatile 1960s.

Held up as an exceptional Black student, I was conditioned to believe in the myth of my own exceptionalism, to see other Black students' struggles to succeed as a result of their own terrible choices. But white children in my school district weren't inherently smarter. They were reared in homes where their parents had been college educated and where they had access to enrichment programs and private tutors. I also associated discourses around sex and sexuality with this narrative of choice. At thirteen or fourteen, I didn't recognize that even if the doctrine of abstinence is ineffective at curtailing early parenthood, youth who have opportunities to talk about sex, to travel to conferences and go on mission trips, at least know that there is a world beyond their front door, a world they can't get to if they end up as parents before getting out of high school. These kinds of opportunities to travel and explore were scarce in my working-class community, where most Black folks had limited resources. But my close proximity to middle-class white youth put me in a position to culturally eavesdrop on my white friends, even though I didn't have the experiences they had. I knew the possibilities of those experiences existed. What I learned from watching white kids who were set up to succeed while Black kids were set up to fail, even in matters of intimacy, was that sexual self-regulation was critical to my success. It took me being a grown woman to recognize all the ways that systems of white supremacy regulate our intimate lives, too.

Black girls and Black women, particularly those who have

had any sustained encounter with Christianity, are often immobilized by the hyperregulation of their sexuality from both the church and the state. These messages about excessive and unregulated Black flesh that converge from both the nation-state and the church form a double helix of sexual ideas that form the core of cultural ideas about Black sexuality. These messages constitute a critical strand in a sticky social web that immobilizes Black women caught at the intersections of race, class, gender, and lack of access to normative modes of sexual behavior. Black feminist scholar Patricia Hill Collins refers to this sticky web as a matrix of domination, a sociological term for the way social systems of power converge to impede Black women's agency and structural well-being. Far too often the result of trying to extract ourselves from these webs, which immobilize us until all of the life is drained from us, is that we leave critical pieces of ourselves behind. Black women are often robbed of our agency to build healthy intimate lives. These systems don't crush every Black woman, but they do retain pieces of flesh, bone, and spirit.

When you are free enough to run away, you run. It makes no earthly sense to go back and do battle with the system for the fragments of yourself that remain. We are taught to be grateful that we "made it," no matter what we had to leave behind.

This is why Black women's self-help literature is obsessed with the question of "how to be whole again."

For my grandmother, my very successful regulation of my sexual desires read like a wholly unhealthy inhabitation of my own Black woman body. I was a fully grown woman, but my theology and thought process around sex was adolescent and retrograde. Grandmama pushed me to articulate a version of my selfhood that would force me to bring my whole self to the table and prioritize my pleasure.

"Girl," Grandmama said while gesturing mischievously toward her nether regions, "I had good stuff." (I repeat: No one ever wants to know this about their grandmother.) She wanted me to own the fact that my "stuff" was "good stuff," too. My grandmother's indecent proposal constituted a critical and intimate dissent from the wholesale American demonization of Black women's sexuality. To justify enslaving, raping, and breeding Black women and girls, white Americans created a mythos around Black women's sexuality. They cast us as sexually insatiable, unrapeable, licentious, and dirty. Today, Black women still experience much handwringing around owning our sexuality. Calling her sexuality and her sexual body parts *good* in the face of these unrelenting social messages suggests that my grandmother had wrested her own sexual subjectivity from the fearsome clutches of Christianity and white supremacy. Or maybe she simply didn't buy in all the way. She, of course, couldn't resist a little inappropriate body commentary as Southern grandmothers are wont to do, telling me "You need to lose a little weight, so he won't have to lift it [my tummy] up to get to it [my stuff]."

The problem is that I still inherently saw my "stuff" as bad, as the source of a temptation so mighty that it could derail my relationship with God and my life goals all at the same time. This is no way to teach sex education to teens, and it is a completely absurd way for grown-ass women to think about sex. Most Christian theology infantilizes women in just this manner. It makes us think that because we are all children of God, God only ever sees us as children. And, as a result, we'll be grown women afraid of embracing our sexuality, approaching it with the ingrained trepidation we learned in our teenage years. I rebuke this foolishness. I am God's child, as I think every human being is. But God knows I'm grown.

The politics of fear and endless rules that we use to (try to) control teenagers is unhealthy but understandable. Advocating that teens delay sex is ultimately about maximizing their life chances by helping them make choices that will benefit them and the future families they hope to build. We could, of course, do a better job of telling teens to do something other than wait. It turns out that my "simple equation" that abstinence would solve teen pregnancy was totally wrong. In places where abstinence is the only form of sex education, teen pregnancy rates are alarming. In places where access to contraception and proper information about birth control is available, teen pregnancy rates have decreased astronomically. What the poor Black girls in my school needed was not the True Love Waits campaign, but rather good information about sex, emotional maturity, and birth control. What was true for my grandmother in the 1950s was true for my Black girl peers in the 1990s: "They just couldn't get the stuff."

Telling grown-ass women that all sex outside of marriage is an affront to God is absolutely ludicrous. Healthy consensual touch is nothing short of holy. But the indoctrination is real, especially if you are invested in being a "good girl," especially if your goal in life is to not "repeat the cycle," to not "become a statistic." These are the kinds of social messages that Black women and girls get about their bodies and the potentially enormous public and personal costs of their sexuality. My mother once mentioned that when she found herself pregnant with me at age eighteen, at *her* grandmother's insistence she had to go up in front of the church and ask for the congregation's forgiveness for getting pregnant out of wedlock. She was ashamed and infuriated because, as she said, "other girls were doing it. They just hadn't gotten caught."

The theology my grandmother offered to me (one very different from her mother's), a theology for grown Black women, was one predicated on dissent from a set of biblical truths and social mores that shamed women, cast female sexuality as bad, dirty, and evil, and suggested that marriage was the only proper context through which women could express their sexual selves. Widowed at the age of forty-two, my grandmother chose to never remarry. She told me that same day, "I would never want to marry again, because I don't ever want some man telling me what groceries I can and can't buy." That was all she said about marriage—that she understood it as men being able to dictate to women how to spend money and how to run a household. Living her own life and being able to raise at least some of her children independent of my grandfather's influence had shown my grandmother that having a male head of household was not, in fact, desirable. In her forthright rejection of conservative evangelicalism on the matter of sex, she modeled for me that Black women had the right to dissent from theologies that didn't serve them well. Black women had the right to a say about their finances, their bodies, the number of children they bore, and the kind of sex they wanted to have. What she offered to me that day was permission to choose for myself.

I wish I could say that I stepped off my grandmother's porch a new woman, ready to own and explore her sexuality. But all her fussing about what I needed to be doing proved no match for the years of shaming and moral panic about sex that I experienced both inside and outside of my community. Four years after that conversation, I came home from church after a particularly guilt-compelling sermon, bagged up all my romance novels, astrology books and manuals, and my vibrator, and threw them in the dumpster. The presence of these items in my apartment were tacit licenses for me to engage and indulge in sinful living, and surely God was not pleased with that. These days, I'm sure that between peals of laughter, God is sitting somewhere, saying, "Girl, bye. I didn't tell you to throw away all those books and that perfectly good vibrator." Live. Learn.

What does it mean when our spiritual and theological systems impede healthy living? This is a question that Black women should begin to ask forthrightly. They should insist fervently on answers among themselves and from their spiritual leaders. We do a kind of violence to ourselves when we shut down our sexuality. It's not so much that I should have had more sex, although I wish I had in my twenties. It's that there are things we come to know about our bodies, our impulses, our likes, our dislikes and desires, when we fully engage the sexual part of ourselves. We go around missing critical knowledge about who we are, or might be, when we act as though sex isn't foundational to who we are.

Also, what does it mean when our theological systems impede our access to a healthy and robust set of spiritual and political practices—practices that should give us life? Let me be a bit mischievous (like my grandmother) and offer you a brief feminist interpretation of one of my favorite Bible stories. In the Black Church, single Black women love to talk about how they are just *waiting on God to send their Boaz.* By Boaz, they are referring to the Old Testament story in the Book of Ruth. Ruth's husband (Naomi's son) had died, and Naomi decided to return to her hometown of Bethlehem. Ruth went with her. To support the two of them, Ruth went to work in the fields, and she was noticed by a well-respected, rich man in town named Boaz, a distant relative of Naomi. Naomi wanted to make sure Ruth could get married again so she would have a partner and a community to provide for her. So the two of them hatched a plot for Ruth to proposition Boaz. Naomi told Ruth to take a bath, get dressed up, and put on some perfume. After Boaz had gotten good and drunk at the barley harvest, Ruth was supposed to go into his tent and, as the Bible says, "lie at his feet" to let him know she was available for marriage. As the story goes, Boaz woke up and found Ruth there, and he decided to marry her right on the spot.

Now, think about it. Does this story make any damn sense? A young woman finds a rich, fine-ass man she wants to marry. So she gets all dressed up, waits for him to get drunk, sneaks (stalkerishly) into his tent, and then *lies at his feet*?! I don't believe it. Not when there is well-documented evidence that the word "feet" in the Old Testament was often a euphemism for genitals! Christian women want their Boaz, but they reject every single part of the process to get him. Ruth and Naomi plotted to trick Boaz into marrying her. Ruth kicked it to him first. She didn't wait on Boaz to ask her out on a date. And I personally think that Ruth did all manner of sexual acts to drunken Boaz in the tent (the kind of shit that made him get up out of his sleep and say "I gotta marry this girl"). But even if you think Ruth simply "lay at his feet" all night, that's a serious sexual proposition.

With the blessing of her elders, Ruth mapped out what she wanted and went after it. She didn't let cultural conventions about chastity, purity, and patriarchy keep her from asking for what she wanted. She also seemed to have a very forthright and embodied sense of her sexuality to help her along. In short form, I'm saying, "Girl, if you want your Boaz, put on your pretty dress and perfume and get your cranial maneuvers together. And then go into the tent and handle your business. But maybe get Boaz's consent before you pop up like that, though."

On her porch that day, my grandmother taught me what it meant for grown women to have an intergenerational gathering and make meaning out of the texts and scripts we have about our lives together. My grandmother did for me what Naomi did for Ruth. She tried to empower me to fight for my happiness by helping me to not be limited by script and convention. She modeled the ways that Black women can build a life for themselves. And sometimes that comes with a willingness to cast aside fear and say no to what others think is best for you, so you can find the courage to say yes to yourself.

There are so many ways that Black women need to free themselves from the strictures of conservative Christian theology. Notice that I didn't say to abandon Jesus and the church if it's important to you. I haven't. But I'm no longer checking my thinking cap at the door. For years, I let Christian preachers convince me that the story of Ruth and Boaz pivoted upon a weird cultural ritual in which men get drunk and then women lie down next to them all night, only to wake up with a marriage proposal the next morning. That shit is just absurd.

We believe a lot of other absurd theologies, too. Many Black Christian girls are seduced by white evangelicalism, because, hell, it seems to be working out so well for white people. I mean, white Jesus helps white people to win a lot. But when my grandmother showed me that I could take a different approach to my theology, that it could be a push and pull, a debate, and even an ongoing set of arguments with God, she freed me up from my investment in being a Christian Goody Two-Shoes. I don't even believe God wants that. The God of Christianity seems to love people who are engaged in all manner of scandals, affairs, and murders. But I digress. We also have an absurd theology of discrimination against LGBTQ people. And far too many churches still believe that women can't be preachers or pastors. The thing we would all do well to remember is that conservative Christian theology was used to enslave Black people. We can use our theology to oppress people or to liberate them. That's our choice.

Sometimes this means that we have to reject the kind of Christian teaching that sets up a false binary between flesh and spirit, mind and body, and sacred and secular. To be Black in the United States is to be taught our flesh is dirty and evil. A liberatory theology for us cannot set us at war with our very bodies. A liberatory theology for women cannot set us at war with the desires for touch, companionship, and connection that well up like deep springs in our spirits. When we hear about how "the heart is deceitful above all things," which is an actual verse, it teaches us to suppress our deepest longings, to not trust our own thoughts and our own counsel. For people who have been enslaved and oppressed because of their race, or gender, or sexuality, such interpretations are dangerous.

I am a professionally trained textual critic, but the Bible isn't any old regular text. It is a text endued with thousands of years of political, social, and cultural power. That means that to wrest a theology for my grown Black woman life from it, I had to bring my fully embodied, unapologetic self to it. My grandmother didn't teach me anything about how to understand the biblical text more critically. She taught me what it meant not to jump out of my own skin just because the Bible said I should be at war on the inside. She offered to me a fully embodied theology of grown Black woman-hood that day, one with its compass set toward freedom. One in which I should embrace the fundamental goodness of all my stuff, both sexual and otherwise. I had to become a fully grown Black woman to receive it, though. In my holy hubris, I had dismissed her as provincial and out-of-pocket. How did she know, in her sanctified country-ness, that sexual pleasure and the freedom to pursue it would be critical to a healthy sense of self? She modeled for me one of the core things Black church girls would do well to remember about Jesus: He fully embodies both the divine and the human. If we spent as much time thinking about how he lived as we do worshipping how he died, our faith would demand that we prioritize a better integration of flesh and spirit, of humanity and divinity, than we do.

The second thing we need to remember is this: The primarily white male theologians who created the systematic theology of evangelical Christianity were trying to make sense of a theology that fit their own lives and their own worldview. This is why so many white Christians can read the Bible and still vote Republican. Because for them, nothing about the Bible challenges the fundamental principles of white supremacy or male domination.

Interpreting the biblical text conservatively has a political function. This political function differs depending on whether you're white or Black. Conservative biblical interpretation became the hallmark of the rise of the religious right, a political force that rose in response to desegregation in the South, and Lyndon Johnson's perceived betrayal of Southern Democrats. Conservative biblical interpretation in Black churches has conversely risen in response to the political evils engineered by the white religious right. White male Christian conservatives used conservative biblical interpretation to pioneer a religious right wing to shore up the machinations of white supremacy in government policy. Black religious conservatives adopted conservative biblical interpretation to inoculate themselves against the massive devastation of these same social policies. Although the social desires (or political goals) of these religious communities are wholly oppositional, the biblical interpretation methods are the same. Obviously, that can't work. If Black women are honest, it hasn't been working for us for a long time.

Perhaps it's time for us to read some other sacred texts alongside the Bible. My grandmother's words are a sacred text to me—a sacred text of country Black girlhood. My mother's words are a sacred text to me—a sacred text of grown Black womanhood. The words of Sojourner Truth, and Alice Walker, and Zora Neale Hurston, and Audre Lorde, and Patricia Hill Collins, and Anna Julia Cooper, and Beyoncé and my homegirls are all sacred texts to me. Black feminism has been a liberatory theology for me in its own right. It has made space for me to bring my spiritual self into the academy and my academic, intellectual self into the spiritual parts of my life. What Black feminism and my grandmother have taught me is that Black women are experts on their own lives and their own well-being. Grandmama taught me that all the sacrifices I was making for middle-class aspirations weren't entirely worth it. That if I made it but I was lonely and miserable, then that was a failure, not a win.

When I first wrote on the Crunk Feminist Collective blog about searching for a new, more liberatory theology of sexuality, the comments section was a nightmare. Many of our readers were not here for the kind of Black feminist theology I was offering. Related to but distinct from womanist theology, what I call Black feminist theology is something that can help sisters who are damn near ready to leave the church just so they can act like grown women with full sex lives in peace. My Black feminist theology is not just focused on what happens in the church, but rather is a call to those of us who are Black feminists to remember that lots of Black women are still quite religious. We need a way to reconcile our feminist politics and our spiritual lives, not only at church or mosque, but at the office, too. Still, a lot of folks at our blog weren't trying to hear it. Some sisters called me "Beelzebub." Seriously. They told me my words were poisonous. One said I had a "reprobate mind" and had been given over to Satan. These angry commenters all agreed that I was not allowing myself to be led by the Holy Spirit. All of those sisters, many of whom had been celibate for years and years, were scared as hell. What if I was right? This is not about right and wrong, though. This is about what freedom means. This is about not standing by idly or, even worse, participating as white evangelicals and their enthusiastic Black counterparts hand to us a theology that does the dirty work of racism, patriarchy, and homophobia. Even when Black people were enslaved and it was illegal for them to "read the word for themselves" (as Black Christians love to say), they knew that God was nothing if not freedom. I believe that because of all the oppressions that we've experienced, Black girls have unique visions of freedom. I believe those visions are God-given, however you understand God, even if you simply worship, to paraphrase Alice Walker, the "God you found in yourself." Freedom is my theological compass, and it never steers me wrong.

Recently, a twenty-three-year-old Black woman who worked at a university where I had flown in to deliver a talk gave me a ride to the airport. My talk was about what it would mean to move beyond respectability, the subject of my first book, *Beyond Respectability: The Intellectual Thought of Race Women*, and how to embrace a feminist politic that was insistent, loud, demanding, ratchet, and unapologetic. On the hour-long drive into the airport, my Black girl chauffeur told me "I hate to make you work, but since I have you in the car, I'm wondering . . ." Anybody who flies to places and speaks for a living often dreads this encounter of being trapped in the car with a stranger and their questions. But I give Black girls a lot of rope, so I listened. "Well," she began, "how have you found that Black men respond to this discussion about feminism?"

There it was—the question that haunts so many Black girls. "Will feminism fuck up my love life?" She went on to offer some context for the behavior of Black men on her campus who were decidedly race-first in their analysis. But I got the subtext—"Will any brother ever love me if I go down this path? Cuz it's not looking too promising." She was a church girl with very religious parents. I took the opportunity to share with her some of my struggles to reconcile faith and feminism. She and I talked about approaching the Bible not as a rule book, but perhaps as a cultural library of texts that recount the journeys of a series of ancient human beings with God, an approach I learned from reading theologian and writer Brian McLaren. When I floated this "radical" idea, she immediately shot back, "But what about repentance, though?"

By this she meant what about the demand that we must always atone for our sins, and always seek to "turn from our wicked ways." Drawing on McLaren's work, I explained to her, "Repentance to me means 're-think.' That's literally what it means. To think again and to think in a different direction."

It was one of those encounters steeped in serendipity, one of those opportunities to talk to a younger version of myself and to share the things I wish someone had said to me when I was twenty-three, anxious as shit, and freaked the hell out. "But, what will my mother say?" she asked. We talked about how to navigate one's own needs as a grown woman, even when they diverge in critical ways from the desire of so many Black girl overachievers to please the women who raised us. I told this Black girl that if I could tell my younger self anything, it would be to "chill out." That is what my grandmother had been trying to tell me.

And that's what my grandmother cosmically sent a homegirl to tell me years later when I was finally ready to listen. Yet again, I required a homegirl hem-up. Robin and I had become friends at just about the moment when I was exhausted from trying not to show up to my own life. Even after the Great Porch Intervention, I went on with these bouts of sexual self-torture for years, declaring celibacy, falling off the wagon, and then declaring it once again. By the time I finished with my Ph.D. program and arrived at my first job, I was sexually frustrated in the worst way and desperate for a new way to think. During a conversation with Robin, I shared that it had been several years since I had had any sex at all. Appalled at the absurdity of my quest for "holiness," she pinned me with a Black-girl look that said I was being foolish and told me, "God knows you want to get some." God knows I did. So I did.

I don't know what changed. Maybe, with all of my schooling complete, I felt like I really had made it. Maybe my twenty-eight-year-old body would no longer be denied. Maybe I had been looking for permission and I was ready to listen. Robin's resistance to the crazy-making sexual politics of the church helped, too. She was brave enough to see past all the ways that church and culture told Black women "no." She was brave enough to go in search of her own "yeses." Brave enough to trust that God does, in fact, have some yeses for grown-ass women. Brave enough, like my grandmother was, to recognize that all the stuff we're made of God calls "good." Because of her, I braved the roiling waters of my own heart and decided to, for once, stand on my own side. Spiritual attitude adjustment complete, I set out on a quest for the good stuff.

ORCHESTRATED FURY

Respectability politics died the day Michelle Obama showed up to her last official engagement as First Lady with a thrown-together ponytail-bun combination and a facial expression fit for a funeral. She looked flawless as always. She also looked fed up and ready to go. Respectability politics, the belief that Black people can overcome many of the everyday, acute impacts of racism by dressing properly and having education and social comportment is, first and foremost, performed as a kind of sartorial prerogative. What I mean is that your fashion choices are subject to great scrutiny. Black people are taught to care how they look and how their children look. If you see a little Black girl out in public with her hair unkempt—her parts unintentionally jagged, her edges unsmoothed, her ponytails askew, or her hair ornaments not in their proper place—you can be assured that there is some Black woman somewhere asking, "Who does that baby belong to?"

Black women's hairstyles are their own cultural vocabulary, which change depending on mood, life circumstance, and who exactly will be seeing us on any given day. Mrs. Obama's hairstyle was the kind you put together after you'd been up all night packing and it's time to get your shit, leave the keys on the counter, and go. It's not public hair. It is not hair given to inaugural pomp and circumstance. It is everyday Black-girl hair. We learn this complex hair vocabulary as we sit perched, often for hours, between the knees of mothers, aunties, and hairstylists, trained and untrained, from babyhood forward.

Every night, my mother painstakingly parted my hair and greased my scalp, and then plaited or rolled my hair for ease of styling in the morning. The next morning, I would sit between her legs while she parted my hair into three or four neat sections, affixed rubber bands to the tops of each section, and then twisted my ponytails. She finished by tying ribbons at the tops and snapping barrettes on the ends. At the end of each day, she would fuss and scold when I came home with those same barrettes missing and ponytails askew and unraveled after "ripping and running and not being careful" at recess. At age twelve, when my mother finally decided it was time for me to get a perm, my hairdresser, Mrs. Earline, asked my mother "Are you sure?" And, later, when Mom came to pick me up with my newly permed, silky tresses, Mrs. Earline said, "I prayed over this baby's head. When I didn't see any hair on the comb as I worked it through, I knew the Lord was saying it was going to be alright." Maintaining my head of long, thick hair was a community project.

At age fifteen, when I accompanied my mother and her three sisters to see the movie premiere of *Waiting to Exhale*, I knew what it meant, then, when Bernadine, after being newly separated from her cheating husband, went to the hairdresser and asked her stylist to chop off nearly every inch of her beautiful, luxurious mane. Even though I didn't have the emotional maturity to understand the devastation of losing a marriage, I knew how much effort it took to grow that length and thickness of hair and keep it beautiful. I knew how much Black women and girls envied having long, thick hair in a world where white women's ability to grow and re-grow hair like weeds was the standard of beauty. Chopping it all off meant she was going through something exceedingly terrible.

My social media and text feeds lit up the moment we got a good look at Mrs. Obama's last inauguration hairdo. Throughout her two terms as first lady, and particularly in the second term, Mrs. Obama's public hair was always long and flowing, with unique kinds of cuts and styles. Black women were culturally obsessed with both her fashion choices and her hair. Was it permed or was it natural? Was she rocking bangs? Who was her stylist and what were they doing to give her hair all that bounce and body? How were Malia and Sasha wearing their hair? These questions are all forms of cultural assessment that Black women and girls do with other Black women and girls. Though sometimes it can morph into mean-girlness, in Mrs. Obama's case, our running cultural commentary about her hair was one of seeing her and feeling seen. It meant that there were Black girls in the White House with hair—challenges, and woes, and triumphs—just like us. So when I saw her hair on her last day, it was clear that she had not spent hours in a stylist's chair getting her 'do done just right. Presumably, she would have wanted to be a fashion stunner for her final formal public appearance. Instead, this bona fide fashion icon showed up to the inauguration of Donald Trump with a quick and convenient on-the-go 'do, and what looked like a good church dress she had pulled from the closet. Certainly, she may simply have been gracious in letting Melania have her moment. But there was also something about the refusal to perform the public standard—a standard that Mrs. Obama had herself set—that marked an unceremonious ending.

Her hair was a signal to the world that what we were about to witness was some bullshit. She knew it. We knew it. "Do y'all see this shit?" that hair asked of all of us who were watching or deliberately not watching our complicated American homeland being placed in the hands of a mentally unwell fascist. Like the rest of us, she might have to accept it, but she didn't have to like it. The "I-refuse-to-be-botheredness" of that ponytail evinced rage of both the eloquent and the elegant varieties. It wasn't so much about the actual hairstyle. A bun or ponytail can be elegant and appropriate. It was the combination of this kind of informal updo with a dress that was pretty, but also unremarkable, that signaled a kind of pulling back, a disengagement, with the American public. Mrs. Obama didn't throw her middle fingers up at the system that had just elected Donald Trump. However, the subtlety in her refusal of pomp and circumstance belied a deep disdain for the way in which the American people had rejected her work, and that of President Obama, by installing his nemesis—a man who had started a whole movement questioning his citizenship—in the White House.

Respectability politics are at their core a rage-management project. Learning to manage one's rage by daily tamping down that rage is a response to routine assaults on one's dignity in a world where rage might get you killed or cause you to lose your job. Mrs. Obama had to learn this lesson quickly, and on the national stage, after being accused and publicly caricatured as an Angry Black Woman when Mr. Obama ran for his first term. She chose to channel her energy into slaying the American public in another way, by offering an impeccable standard of fashion to a watching world. Sometimes that is what Black women do when we can't give in to the murderous levels of rage we feel at the indignities we experience. We can't kill. But we can *slay*.

Rage is a fundamentally more reasonable response to America's cultural investment in the disrespect of Black women than being respectable. That's why it's damn near impossible for rage and respectability to reside in the same place. On her last day, Mrs. Obama didn't sublimate the rage over Trump and his wife to the province of *the slay*. She simply refused. Rage is a kind of refusal. To be made a fool of, to be silenced, to be shamed, or to stand for anybody's bullshit. It is a refusal of the lie that Black women's anger in the face of routine, everyday injustice is not legitimate. Black women's rage is a way of looking these mischaracterizations in the face and responding, "You got me *all the way* fucked up."

This is what I heard—what I *felt*—when I saw Mrs. Obama's

ponytail. Having had her anger hyperpoliced since 2007, when her husband announced his candidacy, on her very last day on the job Mrs. Obama became, as comedy writer Damon Young might say, "fuck-deficient." Since the definition of respectability politics is that you absolutely give a fuck (because you have to) about what white folks and everybody else thinks, respectability politics and fuck-deficiency pretty much *cannot* coexist in the same body.

Audre Lorde, the first writer to offer a Black feminist theory of anger, famously argued in "The Uses of Anger: Women Responding to Racism," the essay that I always keep close at hand, that "Women of Color in america have grown up within a symphony of anger, at being silenced, at being unchosen, at knowing that when we survive, it is in spite of a world that takes for granted our lack of humanness, and which hates our very existence outside of its service. And I say *symphony* rather than *cacophony* because we have had to learn to orchestrate those furies so that they do not tear us apart." Black women's rage is a kind of orchestrated fury. Lorde went on to say, "We have had to learn to move through them and use them for strength and force and insight within our daily lives. Those of us who did not learn this difficult lesson did not survive. And part of my anger is always libation for my fallen sisters." Michelle Obama's negotiation of Trump's inauguration, the manner in which she both expressed her disdain but kept it respectful at the same time, was nothing short of symphonic.

Black folks codified the ideology of respectability in the decades following Reconstruction after the federal government, helped along by indifferent white Northerners, left newly freed Black folks in the South to fend for themselves against the terroristic whims and fancies of angry white Southerners, who were still licking their wounds over their Civil War loss. Women and men like Anna Julia Cooper, Mary Church Terrell, W.E.B. Du Bois, and Booker T. Washington reasoned that if Black folks learned to work hard, educate themselves, and stay out of trouble, white people would see that we were good, respectable people, *human beings*, worthy of both citizenship and protection. Initially, respectability politics was a survival strategy in the face of the massive potential for violence. It was a conservative strategy but an imminently reasonable one for nineteenth- and early twentieth-century Blacks faced with high rates of illiteracy, housing and job insecurity, and cyclical influxes to the North of Black folks looking to make a better life. Showing these Black people how to present a respectable image became a key strategy in securing their survival in hostile and violent conditions.

The problem with all provisional strategies, particularly when they begin to work for the exceptional few, is that they rise to the level of ideology. Soon, Black folks began to blame other Black people for bringing the race down. The Respectables, as I like to call them, claimed that our refusal to practice chastity and piety and avoid crime led to our low esteem among white people. Taken to its extreme form, respectability politics will net you Black people who don't love Black people. Ben Carson and Clarence Thomas are the chiefs among these anti-Black Judas types.

But the Obamas themselves practiced and subscribed to a mild, everyday politics of respectability, too. During an infamous commencement address at historically Black Bowie

State University in 2013, the First Lady critiqued the propensity among Black youth who had been taken in by the lure of celebrity. "Today, instead of walking miles every day to school, they're sitting on couches for hours, playing video games, watching TV. Instead of dreaming of being a teacher or a lawyer or a business leader, they're fantasizing about being a baller or a rapper." This is the language of respectability. It comes from the same place as Sunday sermons that wag fingers at young men to pull up their pants. It comes from the same place as Barack Obama's unique penchant for telling Black men to be good fathers to their children, a message he never felt compelled to share with predominantly white audiences. The ways the Obamas engaged Black audiences during their time in the White House were filled with what we might call the everyday respectability politics of our parents and grandparents, who implored us: "Act like you got some sense," and "Don't make me have to come up to that school."

The Respectables' credo is two-fold: You have to be twice as good to get half as far, and Never let 'em catch you slippin'. (But the Respectables ideally would say this in completely proper English, without my Hip Hop–era remix.) This sounds like good sense. It sounds like Black people taking on the very high levels of personal responsibility that those on the right love to talk about so much. But it doesn't acknowledge that when you are twice as good, white folks will resent you for being better. And all human beings deserve at least a few slips. It's inhuman to demand otherwise.

When we saw the Obamas exit their caravan and walk down the streets of Washington, D.C., smiling and waving on January 20, 2009, these guiding principles reached great commandment status. We felt our ancestors smiling. We felt new possibilities taking shape for our children. For once, America had let us win. The project of respectability had triumphed. It had proven that if Black people would simply get educated, be upstanding and respectable, and work hard, they could be absolutely anything—even president.

But the respectability project was particularly burdensome for Michelle Obama. She was policed and critiqued from head to toe by every community—white, Black, and in-between. When she turned inward to focus on her children, a safe stance that made her more palatable to broad American audiences, white feminists expressed disdain for her embrace of the "mom-in-chief" role, calling it antifeminist. They conveniently forgot that their ancestors had long claimed ladyhood uniquely for themselves, refusing, to the great chagrin of Black women, to acknowledge that sisters of a darker hue were ladies, too. However, Black women refused to cede the volatile turf of American ladyhood to white women, taking to public outlets to remind white women that it was a privilege for a Black woman to be able to *just* focus on raising her kids. This battle to define ladyhood for ourselves, and to access its protections, was longstanding. I think again of Ida B. Wells being ejected from the ladies' car after she had refused to sit in the smoky, filthy, segregated colored car of the train. A few years later, Anna Julia Cooper wrote about needing to use the bathroom at a train station. When she approached the door, each was marked with a sign, one reading "for ladies," and the other "for colored." Which sign should she, a consummate colored lady, choose?

To be a Black woman is to be always confronted with these kinds of profane distinctions, to be asked to choose between your race and your gender. Black social life in the nineteenth century was marked for Black women by a lack of access to the protections of ladyhood, and by a steadfast refusal among white people to even make gender distinctions among Black people. Those ideas shaped the way in which Michelle Obama was both perceived and policed. There was a minor public outcry when she took her official White House portrait in a sleeveless dress. And there was the time U.S. Congressman Jim Sensenbrenner referred to her as having a big butt. One of the perks of being a lady is not being subject to people's lewd, thinly veiled sexual commentaries. Michelle Obama enjoyed no such perks. It also bears noting that white people's regulation of Black women's bodies in the public sphere is one reason that Black people have been obsessed with outward appearance. Michelle Obama's ascent to ladyhood, despite these persisting obstacles, conquered that offensive history, proving that Black women could be the arbiters of American femininity and style, too.

Meanwhile, Melania Trump represented everything that Mrs. Obama did not. During the 2016 campaign, not only were Mrs. Trump's educational credentials in question and her open brand of sexuality deemed antithetical to respectable American ladyhood, but in her Republican National Convention speech, she *plagiarized Michelle Obama*. Yet this is the couple that the American people chose to succeed the Obamas in the White House. Meanwhile, Melania Trump was allowed to float above criticism, even though she initially refused to live in the White House and to take on the social demands of First Ladyhood. Had Michelle Obama dared to be so resistant, we would never have heard the end of the insults and bellyaching of the American public. But Mrs. Trump is the beneficiary of America's silence.

Of course, on Inauguration Day, Michelle Obama was *put out* with this whole state of affairs. Being compelled by law and custom to hand the mantle over to someone who tried to obtain it by biting your beats is almost too much to bear. But it also is perhaps the most symbolic evidence of the failure of the project of African American respectability.

A Black woman, descended from enslaved people, became the First Lady of a country that historically used Black women's bodies merely to reproduce noncitizens. One of the most unique things about Black women's experiences in this country is that we are the only group of people whose bodies have ever been legally mandated as the place that reproduced noncitizens. Indigenous women were never striving for their children to have American citizenship, but rather sovereignty on their own terms. And Latina immigrant women who are unfairly maligned for giving birth to children on American shores are hated precisely because they, too, can pass on the rights of citizenship to their children, even if they have been denied access to it themselves. It is Black American women whose bodily history is bound up with the burden of reproducing the condition of unfreedom for our children. It, therefore, meant something—possibly even everything—to have a Black woman, descended from these Black women, to ascend to the highest role our nation designates for women (since the presidency still eludes us.)

But by January 20, 2017, as Melania Trump stepped to the

podium in her baby-blue suit, that project had proved itself unsustainable. African American respectability might bring us to the highest office in the land, but it could not ensure any level of long-term respect for Black humanity, Black womanhood, Black manhood, or Black childhood. During the Obama administration unarmed Black men, Black women, and Black children had all been murdered by the police, while most of the offending officers never lost their jobs or freedom. So it made sense that Mrs. Obama showed up looking somber, as if she were attending a funeral.

Maybe Michelle Obama hasn't divested from respectability politics forever. Truth be told, they have served her well. But a well-timed diss can let you know the limitations of a way of thinking or mode of being in the world. If you weren't looking for it carefully, Lady Obama's class and social position might have allowed you to miss her microresistance. In myriad ways Black women daily resist messages that try to shame us into submission or otherwise steal and kill our joy. That dissent doesn't just happen on national stages. Sometimes it goes down in the everyday spaces that Black women frequent, spaces that are rife with misogynoir (a term that specifically refers to hatred of Black women) and that are tasked with the work of disciplining Black women and girls into respectable ladyhood.

My mother was the first to teach me this lesson. She had come to pick me up after I had spent six weeks attending the Upward Bound summer program at a local Black college. This federally funded summer experience for working-class youth was the closest most of us rural and semirural Southern Black children would ever get to going to summer sleepaway camp. For six weeks, we stayed on campus in the dorms, being exposed to what college life might look like, while we spent our days doing math and science enrichment, attending cultural experiences like plays and poetry readings, and taking long-distance field trips. Those programs mattered to single moms like my own, who had big dreams for their children but very few resources.

Together, Mama and I sat at the final Upward Bound banquet, a celebration of our achievements that summer, listening to a local preacher giving the keynote address. He was in the middle of his sermon text, a classic passage from Proverbs, when my mother began shaking her head: "The Bible *says* 'train up a child in the way he should go, and when he is old he will not depart from it.' Some of your children are acting up, and the *Word* says that means y'all aren't doing your jobs." A chorus of "amens" rose up around the room, affirming this conventional "wisdom." But my mother's head continued to shake. Eventually, a clear but quiet "no," formed on her lips. The head shaking drew eyes to our table, so much so that the preacher stopped, looked at her, and said, "You don't agree?" "No." She shook her head again. He said to her, surprised, "Well, that's alright." Murmurs went up around the room, as other mothers looked at my mother curiously, some with disapproval, some with surprise, and maybe, hopefully, at least a few, in relief. Satisfied that her disagreement had been registered, my mother nodded her head, letting him continue.

Later, in the car on the way home, my mom explained, "That verse says, 'When they are *old*, they won't depart from it.' Y'all aren't old yet." Blaming Black mothers for having normal boundary-testing teenagers didn't sit well with my mother, a single mom herself. Her act of solidarity with the other single mothers in the room mattered all the more because my mother was raising a veritable, rule-following, Bible-toting Goody Two-Shoes. But she refused the carrot of thinking herself better than other folks because her own child didn't have the behavior problems or classroom demeanor of some of the other children. Mama knew she was an underdog in a room full of underdogs, and like she has told me on more than one occasion, "I always root for the underdog."

Too often, Black leaders think rooting for Black folks means shaming them into respectability. Southern Black male preachers are masters of propagating sexist common sense to achieve respectable outcomes. On more Sundays than a few, their rhetoric shames single Black mothers for failing to raise their children in traditional nuclear families. But my mother was the first to teach me that we don't have to accept nonsense simply because it is common. I learned that day that sometimes you have to say no, even in a room where everyone else is offering sacrificial "yeses." Those "yeses" were a sacrifice because assenting to one's own public shaming is not an affirmation any Black woman can ever afford. Saying yes to a religious narrative about bad Black mothering that props up an even more pernicious state-based narrative that pathologizes Black mothers costs too much. A Black male preacher asking Black mothers to collude in their own denigration is unholy.

Black church ladies love the Bible verse that says, "Let all things be done decently and in order." My mother was out of order in every respectable sense. She had challenged a preacher—in public. She challenged his biblical interpretation in a culture that believes preachers have a direct, anointed line to God. She dissented from him openly, forthrightly, and unapologetically. This, too, was eloquent rage—against the theological and social machine of respectability. This, too, was orchestrated fury, in the form of a symphonic disruption—a refusal to let "the man of God" use rhetoric to beat up on vulnerable women trying to make a way in the world for themselves and their children. My mama didn't turn over any tables in the temple like her Jesus might have done, but she did cause just enough of a disruption to make clear that an injustice was being done. Eloquent rage isn't always loud, but it is always effective.

Fourteen and a bit nonplussed by my mother's decision to make a scene, I didn't even know you could do something as bold as challenge a preacher. In Southern Black communities, the Great Chain of Being goes something like God, Black Male Preachers, and the Rest of Us. But sometimes the only thing that is in order is to act out of order. To turn up, show out, and disrupt. That preacher was touting a particular order of things, a hierarchy of shame that placed Black women on the bottom. Inherent within his remarks was an indictment of the kinds of Black families in the audience. These were working-class Black people raising children in one of the poorest states in the union. These Black families weren't two-parent, middle-class Black families. There were a few fathers, but mostly there were mothers, grandmothers, aunties, and younger siblings in that room.

Here was the Moynihan Report rearing its ugly head

again. Black mothers, according to Moynihan, were the source of our deepest, most faulty conditions. The roots of Black social wrongness ran deep. They ran to the womb, to the mothers, to the maternal labor that birthed us and made space for us. Parroting the logic of Moynihan, and many Black sociologists who had come before, this preacher argued that the reason that Black children were out of line was that fathers were absent and mothers weren't mothering well. My mother insisted on a different story. And she was willing to be disruptive in order to make that story heard.

This is what anti-Blackness looks like. This is what misogynoir sounds like. The rub is that these mansplaining men think they are *helping*. Moynihan thought his report would help. The preacher thought his sermon would help. But this is the kind of help that will kill you. In the absence of actual structural resources to ameliorate social problems, sermonic shaming and policy blaming is the opposite of help. It constitutes harm. It sounds eerily similar to the kind of shame and blame that undergirds social-welfare policy in the United States. Dog-whistle policies about welfare moms and Hip Hop anthems about greedy baby mamas and sermons about mothers who don't take care of their children all share a common through line—that Black women aren't shit, that they need to be corralled, controlled, and contained. The logic of otherwise disparately placed men—in public policy, in Hip Hop, and in the church—converges on the truth that if Black women would just be better mothers, the state wouldn't be so taxed, our communities would not be in such a shambles, and brothers wouldn't be so short in the pockets. That's a huge minefield of structurally induced hatred to navigate.

What's even more terrible is that we don't just ask Black women to traverse this difficult terrain. Black girls encounter the daily violence of this hateful cultural landscape, too. Remember, there were girls like me, on the way to becoming women, listening on that day, too, to a narrative of what proper ladyhood looked like. I was too invested in being a "good girl" to ever have thought to disrupt the preacher's message myself. But my mother had been a *bad* girl in many ways, a rebel and a teen mom who liked slightly older bad boys. That's how I got here.

Though good behavior has its place, it's the disruptive girls, the loud, rowdy, attitudinal Black girls, and the defiant, quiet, insolent Black girls who expose every day exactly what this system is made of. In September 2015, a school resource officer in South Carolina confronted a high-school student named Shakara for failure to put away her cell phone as she sat at her desk during math class. To be clear, the term "school resource officer" is a just a fancy name for police officers in schools, doing the kinds of jobs that used to be reserved for principals and school counselors. Although she sat quietly at her desk, Shakara held the phone tightly in her hand, defying her teacher's orders to put it away.

At the behest of the Black male teacher, a white male police officer named Ben Fields arrived and began hassling Shakara. She neither ignored him nor responded to him. Instead, Shakara sat quietly, looking straight ahead, exercising her right to remain silent. An arrest would be forthcoming anyway. Very rarely are Black girls read in ways that recognize what their fear might look like. Fields saw only insubordination, and he responded with escalation, grabbing Shakara with such force that he tipped the desk over while she was still seated inside it. From that position, he yanked her body violently out of the desk, creating such momentum that, as he dislodged her body, she collided violently with the wall.

Shakara's classmates looked terrified, even as one lone distressed teenager, a girl named Niya Kenny, stood up and yelled, "What the fuck?! What the fuck?! This can't happen." Niya encouraged her classmates to tape the incident, and later, said, "I was screaming, 'What the F___? What the F____?' Is this really happening? I was praying out loud for the girl."

Cussing and praying. Mixing the profane and sacred together. No one can cuss you out more eloquently than a Black woman can. It might be a stereotype, but it's also a truth. We cuss out of rage, and we pray that the cussing will be enough to get all the rage out. We curse those who trespass against us, and we pray usually that the rage won't win. We curse systems, and we pray for divine help to overcome those very same systems. This is why it is so egregious for preachers to use biblical texts to shame Black women and girls into complying with a system that hates them. Most Black girls and women come to lean on that same holy language for divine help when the system shows up to smash them into a million pieces. Rage and respectability can't exist in the same space. But cussing and praying absolutely can. These forms of expression, themselves tethered to those spaces between disrespect and respectability, hold Black women together when the violence we encounter would otherwise rip us apart.

Shakara and Niya were both arrested for the dubious

charge of "disturbing schools." More than a year later, the charges were dropped, but not before students at the high school held protests in *favor* of the school resource officer getting his job back. Many of the children who protested were Black, because Black children learn early that the best way to survive in a broken system is to go along to get along. If Shakara hadn't persisted in her small but mighty act of rebellion, we might never have seen just how violent the world is toward Black girls who don't immediately comply. Shakara's rage was quiet. But it was no less eloquent, no less clear.

Many, many Black folks, the ones who daily tell their children, "Don't make me come up to that school," were incensed at Shakara. "Why didn't she just put the phone away?" They asked similar questions when, months earlier, Sandra Bland was threatened with tasing and then arrested after challenging a dubious citation by a Texas police officer.

Because respectability is a rage-management project, those invested in Black respectability are often deeply uncomfortable with Black rage. Respectability tells us that staying alive matters more than protecting one's dignity. Black rage says that living without dignity is no life at all. This rage is dangerous because it can't be reasoned with, can't be forced to accept the daily indignities of racism, and more than likely will fight back, rather than fleeing or submitting. The consequence of all these antirespectable choices range from violence to death. Ask Sandra Bland. . . . *My anger is always libation for my fallen sisters.*

To be clear, Black living and Black surviving matters. We can't be dogmatic about the rightness or wrongness of embracing rage or choosing safety. It would be irresponsible for me to tell people to embrace rage and all its consequences when I daily put on a respectable outfit and drive in a solidly middle-class car to a solidly middle-class job. Perfecting the art of respectability in the right moments helped me to make it this far. But the more access I have to halls of power, to places where decisions get made, the more rage I feel. I know how to "count the costs" of my rage, but I wonder if we've learned how to count the costs of our respectability. It makes us emotionally dishonest. It makes us unable to see each other. It causes us to sympathize with the dignity vampires, come to take everything from us while claiming we brought it on ourselves.

Grown Black people resented Shakara's youthful rebellion. Underneath the resentment, clearly people were horrified at the violence. But the view was, "We already know how *they* will treat us. So we can never give them a reason." *Never let them catch you slippin'.* Luckily, Niya's mother had more vision than much of the shortsighted public discourse. After Niya was arrested for "disturbing schools," her mother said, "Looking at the video, who was really disturbing the school? Was it my daughter? Or was it the officer who came into the classroom and did that to the young girl?" Shakara's silence in the face of such violence, and Niya's loud wailing of distress and disruption came to help us. These Black girls asked us to be emotionally honest about how fucked up this world is. They gave us an opportunity, if we would only get in touch with our rage, with the righteousness of it, to imagine a world in which two grown men could figure out a dignified and reasonable way to get a teenage girl to put away her phone. Suppressed rage will cause us to accept gratuitous violence as a necessary evil. Expressed rage offers us an opportunity to do better.

Two grown men, one Black and one white, one a teacher and one an officer, colluded that day to terrorize two Black girls, and a room full of mostly Black students, into submission. And only the power of Black girls refusing to bow down to this unprincipled show of force alerted the nation to the problem of how Black girls get treated in schools. After she was arrested, Niya left school in pursuit of her GED. Because Shakara was in the foster-care system, her anonymity was protected and it's not clear what happened to her. Niya became another of the disproportionate number of Black girls who are suspended every year compared to their white counterparts. Her contact with the legal system also means that her act of solidarity made her one more Black student forced into what Monique Morris has called the "school-to-confinement pathways" that dog Black girls for the entirety of their educational lives.

Rage is costly. And its costs are directly proportional to the amount of power any given woman or girl has when she chooses to wield it.

But Black women's rage also builds movements. Black Lives Matter. This is the most eloquent statement of rage to come out of Black communities in a generation. Three Black women began proclaiming this simple truth on July 13, 2013, after George Zimmerman was acquitted of killing Trayvon Martin. The entire narrative of the Zimmerman trial had become a story about Black women and rage. Much of the trial decision seemed to rely on the testimony of Trayvon Martin's good friend Rachel Jeantel. He had been on the phone with Rachel just as Zimmerman started to stalk him around the neighborhood. Rachel heard the initial moments of the confrontation before her phone went dead. And when she took the stand on Trayvon's behalf, Rachel was all hood solidarity and unpolished Black-girl attitude. Her rage over the killing of her friend was apparent, but because she had a speech impediment, and little investment in taking the stand to relive the trauma of hearing her friend be murdered, the inelegance of her speech made her rage seem less eloquent. But it was abundantly, expressly clear that she was mad at losing her friend, and mad at the farce of a trial that eventually acquitted Zimmerman. All us Black girls who love bigheaded Black boys as friends and brothers and cousins were mad.

That very same night, Patrisse Cullors, Alicia Garza, and Opal Tometi got together on social media and began proclaiming "#BlackLivesMatter." Those words became even more salient on August 9, 2014, when Ferguson, Missouri, police officer Darren Wilson picked a fight with Michael Brown and his friend Dorian Johnson as they walked in the middle of the street within a small apartment complex on Canfield Drive. Wilson pulled his gun and shot Mike Brown multiple times, claiming afterward that Brown tried to grab his gun. After residents stood vigil for four and a half hours as Mike Brown's body lay in the street, the next iteration of the movement was born.

Individualized acts of eloquent rage have limited reach. But the collective, *orchestrated fury* of Black women can move the whole world. This is what the Black Lives Matter movement has reminded us. There is something clarifying about Black women's rage, something essential about the way it drills down to the core truth. The truth is that Black women's anger is not the problem. "For it is not the anger of Black women," Lorde tells us, "which is dripping down over this globe like a diseased liquid. It is not [our] anger which launches rockets . . . missiles, and other agents of war and death." "Anger," she said, "is an appropriate response to racist attitudes." #AudreLordeTaughtMe

We live in a nation that does everything to induce our rage while simultaneously doing everything to deny that we have a right to feel it. American democracy is as much a project of suppressing Black rage as it is of legitimizing and elevating white rage. American democracy uses calls for civility, equality, liberty, and justice as smoke screens to obscure all the ways in which Black folks are treated uncivilly, unequally, illiberally, and unjustly as a matter of course. Had Darren Wilson been just a bit more "civil," Mike Brown might very well be alive.

The lie we are told is that white rage and white fear are honest emotions that preserve the integrity of American democracy. More often than not, we keep learning that white rage and white fear are dishonest impulses that lead us toward fascism. White rage and white fear are reactions to perceptions among white people that their power might be slipping away. Black rage and Black fear are fundamentally more honest, because they are reactions to the violence of white supremacy. When Black women are the collective arbiters and organizers of Black rage, it is inherently more inclusive. By proclaiming that Black Lives Matter, the leaders of the Movement for Black Lives (M4BL) have been insisting that the American democratic project become as inclusive as it claims to be. White supremacist gaslighting insists that what the statement really means is "only Black lives matter." But that is willful ignorance on the part of folks who refuse to see that the conditions that prompted the proclamation in the first place were conditions that tried to assert that Black lives didn't matter, that they were disposable, and that Black communities didn't deserve justice. Black women, therefore, stood up and said, "We *matter*." *Too. Also.* I simply refuse to believe that white people don't know this.

Whether we are at work, at church, at school, in court, in the halls of government, or in the streets, the rage of Black women and girls does the necessary work of pushing American democracy forward, of exposing its flaws, of dramatizing its injustices, of taking its violent beatings. Black women's rage isn't always healthy, particularly when we turn it on ourselves or on our children. But when we turn it outward and focus it on the powers that would crush us into submission and give back to us a mangled image of ourselves, Black women's rage is a kind of power that America would do well to heed if it wants to finally live up to its stated democratic aims.

WHITE-GIRL TEARS

The problem with the 2016 presidential election is simple: White feminists did not come get their people. Who are the people of white feminists? Other white women. Until the election of Donald Trump, very few Americans, beyond political scientists and analysts, paid attention to the fact that white women have a long history of voting predominantly for Republican candidates in presidential elections. In fact, in 2016, 3 percent fewer white women voted for Trump than those who had voted for Mitt Romney in 2012. That's a significant political shift in one election cycle. But when we woke up on November 9, 2016, to discover that white women were not interested in forming a president in their own image, suddenly we began to train our eyes more heavily on white women, trying to understand what the hell was going on.

As I made clear earlier, I have always known of white women's great capacity to be treacherous. But I did not know that they suffered a far more acute version of a problem that white feminists have for decades diagnosed Black women with having: For white women, their race comes before their gender. See, this tendency to put race before gender does not surprise me with Black women. We grow up in a world that only secondarily acknowledges our girlhood and our womanhood. We grow up being denied the protections of femininity that are always afforded to white women. And because anti-Blackness is so palpable, it's easy if you aren't paying attention to miss the very sexist ways that racism can present itself. Most racial stereotypes of Black women—that they are sexually insatiable, unrapeable, and prone to having a bunch of babies they can't take care of, are gendered stereotypes. But most of us don't learn to identify the problem as one rooted in racism *and* sexism. This is a problem that Black feminist organizers and intellectuals have been attuned to since the very beginning. But I simply didn't know that white feminists had a version of this problem, too. Namely, white women's voting practices tell us that they vote with the party that supports their racial issues, even though this means voting with a party that hates women as a matter of public policy.

On the day after Trump's inauguration, white women took over America, to the tune of more than three million protestors. It is the biggest feminist action ever recorded. But it was hard to see the outraged cries of all these white women, many of whom had failed to *get their people*, as anything other than a public profusion of white-lady tears. White girls usually cry white-lady tears after they have done something hella racist and then been called out by the offended party for doing so. To shift blame and claim victimhood, they start to cry. The world falls apart as people rush to their defense. All knowledge of the fact that they are the ones who caused the problem escapes the notice of everyone except the person or people they disrespected. It's a phenomenon that Black folks know well.

Recently, at a campus lecture I gave, a young Black man told me of an incident where a white female student who he thought was a friend called him a nigger. When he expressed deep offense at her racism, she started crying. He wanted to report her to campus authorities, but felt that given his race, size, and stature, he would not be believed. He felt he would be cast as the aggressor. So he walked away and let it go.

I, too, have experienced white women become aggressively angry at public lectures when I give talks. Recently, I received an award from a national women's organization for my work as a feminist activist. In my remarks, I spoke briefly about the ways the Clinton crime bill had harmed Black communities and men in my own family. As I walked off stage, an older white feminist, a judge, shook with anger as she disagreed with my analysis of the crime bill. I told her that perhaps my analysis could have been more precise, but that the gist of my point about Clinton and the explosion of the prison industrial complex was in fact, correct. She moved further into my personal space, as her face became red, and her voice shook. All of these are cues of physical aggression, and if you're Black, they are signs that somebody is ready to fight. She didn't cry, but I certainly wanted to make her cry. The comfort she felt in physically advancing on a stranger and expecting not to have any clapback for it is a comfort and a privilege that only white women have.

What that white lady judge didn't know is that I eat white-lady tears for breakfast, lunch, and dinner. So it made sense that on the day of the Women's March I skipped it and went to my girl's spot for a very Black brunch in Brooklyn. Watching white women take it to the streets to protest an election outcome that was a result of white women's powerful voting bloc felt like an exercise in white-lady tears if I ever saw one, and I knew I couldn't be trusted to act right amidst a sea of pink pussy hats and white women struggling to understand what intersectionality means.

But I felt conflicted. On the one hand, I wanted to be in the streets helping women make feminist history. It feels really important in this moment to make clear that feminism is a multiracial project. Feminism doesn't belong to white women. When cries arose in the weeks following the election for a Million Women's March, I was skeptical and annoyed. Black women had already had such a march in 1997. Though the organizers of this march scrambled and recovered, re-branding the event the Women's March and placing several women of color at the helm, I decided that I would sit this particular march out. My conflict arose, though, because even though I want white women to learn with a quickness about the many other modes of womanhood that exist out-side of white womanhood, I also understand the power of a unified front.

The election of Trump, a man who had admitted on tape to sexually assaulting women, women who were presumably white, suggests that 2016 is the moment white women ran squarely up against the limits of white-lady tears as a form of political capital. White-lady tears might seem not to be a big deal, but they are actually quite dangerous. When white women signal through their tears that they feel unsafe, misunderstood, or attacked, the whole world rises in their defense. The mythic nature of white female vulnerability compels protective impulses to arise in all men, regardless of race.

I think here of the white-girl rapper travesty that is Iggy Azalea. This Australian white girl built her career by mimicking the accent and cadence of Black girls in Atlanta, Georgia. She was helped along in this regrettable experiment in cultural appropriation by Atlanta rapper T.I. In late 2014, Iggy Azalea dismissed Black female rapper Azealia Banks's claims that America appropriates Black culture by engaging in what Banks called "cultural smudging." In the midst of the racial uproars of 2014—the killing of Michael Brown and Tamir Rice and the refusal of the Ferguson, Missouri, prosecutor to indict Officer Darren Wilson—Banks had called out Iggy for profiting off of Black culture but not speaking out about Black pain. When, days later, Banks followed up in an interview about this longstanding problem of cultural appropriation—think jazz, rock 'n' roll, blues, and blue-eyed soul—Iggy dismissed Banks as a bully who had little success because of her attitude. Rap legend Q-Tip, from A Tribe Called Quest, stepped in to give Iggy a history lesson on Twitter. It was not long before rapper T.I. defended his protégé Iggy by saying that many Black people had a "paranoid, 'All White People Wanna Steal Our Shit'" mentality. Clearly T.I.'s arguments are reductive and ludicrous.

Black people have every right to be upset about the long history of cultural appropriation in this country. The fact that Iggy's career took off at a moment in Hip Hop when Black girls could barely find a record deal (Nicki Minaj being the exception) suggests that our fears and anger about white girls taking up space to which they are not entitled are well-founded.

During these same years, we have endured everyone from Miley Cyrus to Taylor Swift to Katy Perry parroting the sounds and idioms of Hip Hop in their music, while disrespecting Black women in the process. There was the time that Katy Perry rocked corn rows with her front edges gelled down (a hair style that is undeniably specific to Black women) in the music video for her song "This Is How We Do" while pursing her lips, with her head cocked to the side, to impersonate what she thinks attitudinal, edgy Black girls look and sound like. Then there was the time Taylor Swift crawled between the legs of several Black girls twerking in her video "Shake It Off." Let me also note that phrases like "this is how we do" and "shake it off" are themselves Black cultural sayings, indigenous to the Hip Hop generation.

Miley Cyrus even infamously invited Black women with huge posteriors on stage to twerk with her when she was trying to emerge from the good-girl gloss of her old Disney character Hannah Montana. Using the logic of white supremacy to her advantage, she figured that the closer she put her skinny, no-ass-having self to Black women's thick and voluptuous bodies, the easier it would be for people to accept her as a sexually active, slightly vulgar, grown woman. Black women's bodies became critical to this performance of grown womanhood because Miley knew (at least implicitly) that Black women's bodies are already coded as hypersexual and excessively vulgar, and this was everything she wanted to be.

Of late, Cyrus says she has moved away from Hip Hop because, as she told John Norris at *Billboard*, "It was too much 'Lamborghini, got my Rolex, got a girl on my cock'—I am so not that." Now that Hip Hop had rescued her from the stultifying demands to perform pure, chaste white Southern femininity, she was ready to throw it out like a used-up washrag. Of course, Hip Hop had been misogynist for more than three decades when Cyrus thought to use it to add an edge to her image. The ability to take on and peel off the parts of Black culture that you like at will is exactly what is meant by the term "white privilege." And while culture sharing is fine, white people have proven that they have a problem sharing. White people don't share. They take over. They colonize. They claim shit as their own and then accuse others of being territorial and retrograde for pointing out these aggressive borrowing practices that shape white culture. It's wrong to use Black aesthetics, Black cultural vernaculars, and Black dance in your videos without any kind of citation or homage.

Beyond the culture wars, there's a whole political infrastructure designed to protect the sanctity of white women's fears and tears. White women's complicity and participation in state violence toward Black people has a long and sordid history. In 1892, after the local lynching of three Black men, Memphis journalist Ida B. Wells wrote an editorial calling out white men for the lynching. She wrote, "Nobody in this section of the community believes that old threadbare lie that Negro men rape white women. If Southern men are not careful, a conclusion might be reached which will be very damaging to the moral reputation of their women." One of the lynched men, Thomas Moss, was Wells's good friend; he was married with a family, and he was a respected business-man. He and his business partners had, in fact, been lynched for running a successful grocery store that competed with a local white grocer. Once Wells saw the economic logics at play, she stopped believing the myth propagated by white su-premacists, that Black men were running amok raping white women.

Wells also sought to call out the complicity of white women in this racial terror propagated against Black men. Not only weren't they victims, but they were often engaging in consensual, though illicit, sexual relationships with Black men. Sometimes these women would cry rape when they were caught in the act. Sometimes the white men in their lives would cry rape for them. These white women's tears proved deadly for Black men and Black communities. Mean-while, the white men who were outraged over the rape of white women often raped Black women with impunity. Black men, too, were often victims. In a world where telling a white woman "no" could lead to as many consequences as telling her "yes," surely the social conditions were not ripe for any Black body to freely consent to interracial liaisons.

Conveniently enough, white men didn't begin to propa-gate the myth of Black male rapists until after the Civil War. During the war, when they left their wives and daughters on plantations with these same Black men, there were few to no accusations of sexual assault. But after the war, suddenly (we are to believe), white men's outsized outrage and paranoia over the safety of white women was about actual crimes Black men were committing rather than about white men's deep and unbridled rage over losing power. By turning the nation's attention to supposed misdeeds by Black men, white men misdirected attention from the copious amounts of rape they were committing against Black women. Disregard for the bodily autonomy of Black women grew in direct proportion to the social valuation of white femininity. Though this had also been true during slavery, after the Civil War white men used white femininity as an excuse to terrorize newly freed men and women through lynching and rape.

White women's tears are dangerous. Ida B. Wells was run out of Memphis for challenging white women's (and men's) lies about rape, and her newspaper's office was burned to the ground. White men sent a threatening message that they would kill her if she returned to Memphis from her travels up North. Her story demonstrates the extent to which white men were willing to go to protect and promote the narrative of vulnerable white femininity. But it also makes clear just how bothered white men were by the prospect of white women potentially sleeping with Black men. Not only were white men willing to lynch Black men to keep them in line but, in the case of Wells, they were also willing to murder Black women in order to prop up their fantasy about racially pure sexual desire. The desire of white men to regulate white women's intimate desires placed Black people in a cluster-fuck of white terror.

Since the nineteenth century, white feminists have critiqued the ways white men have attempted to sexually regulate their bodies. They have decried the demands for sexual chastity, purity, and monogamy that American culture has presumed to be white women's civic duty. But often the critique stops there. White women never make the leap toward solidarity. That solidarity would be rooted in the fact that the terms and limits of Black women's *and* white women's sexual agency (while certainly not equal in the scope of terror and violence) are both bound up with the project of white supremacy. Far too frequently, white women's notions of antiracist solidarity is defined solely by their willingness to date Black men. I'm coming back to that momentarily.

It is in light of these histories that everyone should be able to understand the complex reactions that Black communities had to allegations against Bill Cosby. The allegations that he raped and sexually assaulted nearly fifty women, most of them white, between the 1960s and the 2000s, were an open secret that most of us deliberately chose to ignore until the cries of his victims got louder and louder. Cosby has denied these allegations. When I initially began hearing about these alleged assaults, my first thought was that Cosby was yet another Black man who secretly found white women more sexually desirable than his gorgeous Black wife, Camille. That was disappointing, but as race-man types go, also rather clichéd. As more and more stories emerged, however, I returned to my default position—I believe women when they say they are raped. No matter their race. That is a hard position to hold, given what Ida B. Wells taught us about the racial and sexual politics of the post-Reconstruction era.

Postslavery, Black manhood was framed primarily in terms

of being a sexual threat to the purity of white womanhood. To find out that there are very compelling reasons to believe that Bill Cosby raped dozens of white women, and began doing so during the racially volatile 1960s, has been hard for many African Americans to accept. If the allegations are true, that would make Cosby as much of a monster as many white people love to think all Black men are. When he was tried in June 2017 for sexually assaulting Andrea Constand, a judge declared a mistrial after a jury failed to reach a verdict. However, the mistrial in his case is no more an assurance of innocence than such mistrials are when the victims are Black men killed by white cops. Too often, the rampant racism of the criminal justice system is used as an excuse for the heinous misogyny and sexism of Black men.

I'm no fair-weather feminist, though. Rape is rape. Sexism is sexism. No matter who commits it. I gave up *The Cosby Show*, a show I loved and had continued to watch, even after Cosby became a moralizing grandfatherly fuckboy who shamed single Black mothers, derided the Black poor, and mocked Black naming practices. In his infamous 2004 Pound Cake Speech, Cosby said, "Women having children by five, six different men. Under what excuse, I want somebody to love me, and as soon as you have it, you forget to parent. Grandmother, mother, and great grandmother in the same room, raising children, and the child knows nothing about love or respect of any one of the three of them." His speech is filled with this shame-and-blame rhetoric, demonizing Black mothers. But I am so used to Black men who blame Black women for our communities' social problems, and to Black elders who believe wholeheartedly in respectability politics, that it seemed a small price to pay to continue to watch *The Cosby Show*. As long as Black women were the targets of Cosby's ire, I could ignore it and continue to enjoy reruns of my favorite sitcom after a long, stressful day. I'm used to brothers being *not quite right* and even *all the way wrong* in their dealings with us. I'm used to seeing their pro- verbial slips showing and loving them anyway. But after it came to light that he might be a vicious sexual predator, any racial solidarity between us fell away. To be clear, I would have made the same choice if the vast majority of his accus- ers had been Black. Some are. But the fact remains that even I sprang into action more readily when I read all of these white women's accounts of his actions, in ways that I had not felt the urgency to do when the targets of his rage were Black. Black men's disdain for Black women is so common that it didn't even occur to me to stop watching his show. White women's tears are powerful.

I wish, however, that white feminists specifically weren't so deliberately oblivious about their privileged status. Fickle feminism won't get us anywhere. Even as Black feminists rallied to denounce Cosby's (alleged) despicable conduct and crimes, there was little to no outrage among white fem- inists when Daniel Holtzclaw, an Oklahoma police officer of Asian and white American descent, was accused of rap- ing thirteen Black women, and was subsequently found guilty of eight of the rapes, in late 2015. While Cosby's accusers commanded mainstream news coverage, Holtzclaw's vic- tims received embarrassingly little media coverage. If, by contrast, a Black police officer had been found guilty of rap- ing multiple white women, this would have been a media circus. This was Ida Wells's point. The alleged vulnerability of white women misdirected critical attention away from the ways in which white men were, in fact, brutalizing and raping Black women and girls. Today, most rapes are intraracial, but white women's perceived vulnerability to crimes at the hands of Black men does untold amounts of harm to Black communities and, in particular, to Black women and children.

When George Zimmerman stalked and killed Trayvon Martin, who was walking home from the corner store in a suburban Florida neighborhood, Zimmerman claimed to be suspicious because Trayvon, a seventeen-year-old Black kid wearing a hoodie, was looking at the houses as he walked home. A Black kid in a hoodie must surely be scoping out these houses, where some white families lived, in order to commit a crime. At Zimmerman's trial, the jury consisted of five white women and one woman of color. As I watched the trial, I wondered which brand of white womanhood would prevail. Would these women act out of their socially constructed fear of Black men in hoodies or would they "transcend" race and identify with Sybrina Fulton, Trayvon's mother, in the unjust loss of her child? After jurors failed to convict Zimmerman on the grounds that he had the right to "stand his ground," it became clear that to the jurors, Trayvon Martin wasn't Sybrina Fulton's baby boy. He was a walking embodiment of white women's worst nightmare. After the trial, Juror B-37, a white woman, gave an interview to Anderson Cooper. Cooper asked the juror why Zimmerman might have found Trayvon to be suspicious, and she responded:

He said he was looking in houses as he was walking down the road. Kind of just not having a purpose to where he was going. He was stopping and starting. But I mean, that's George's rendition of it, but I think the situation where Trayvon got into him being late at night, dark at night, raining, and anybody would think anybody walking down the road stopping and turning and looking, if that's exactly what happened, is suspicious. And George said that he didn't recognize who he was.

Note several things about the juror's answer. She fully agreed with George Zimmerman, that it was reasonable to see Trayvon Martin, a kid walking home in the rain, talking on his phone, as suspicious. As she put it, "anybody would think" this way. By anybody, she means any *white* body. Even if that were true, the larger question is whether any of us would have stopped, followed him, and then shot him to death after doing so. That is the only question. The jurors put themselves fully in George Zimmerman's shoes. They could not find any empathy for the teenage boy walking home with snacks. These women's acquittal of Zimmerman suggested that their primary social priority is white safety, even if it means authorizing lethal force against Black folks who aren't studying them or their white suburban lives in the least. After the Zimmerman trial, white feminists did not call out these jurors. During the trial they did not call on them to exercise integrity, check their white privilege, or act from a place of empathy. White feminism has worked hard to make the world safer for white women, but it has stridently refused to call out the ways that white women's sexuality and femininity is used not just as a tool of patriarchy but also as a tool for the maintenance of white supremacy.

Less than two months before Donald Trump clinched the presidency, a white police officer from Tulsa, Oklahoma, named Betty Shelby shot and killed Terence Crutcher, a forty-year-old unarmed Black man, during a traffic stop. When Shelby shot Crutcher, who was outside of his vehicle at her request, his hands were in the air. As police helicopters covered the scene, they could be heard saying that he looked like "a bad dude." While Shelby's partner used his Taser to subdue Crutcher, who officers say wasn't following commands, Shelby pulled out her gun and shot him, hitting him in the lung. Like many other white police officers who have killed unarmed Black people, her only defense was "I feared for my life." Her fear became a lethal weapon against Terence Crutcher, who was carrying no weapons of his own. Yet again, white feminists did not write think pieces or organize panels asking their white sistren to interrogate the lethal and anti-Black consequences of this "fear." At trial, Betty Shelby was found not guilty of manslaughter, and she went back to work for the Tulsa Police Department.

When Black men show out, Black feminists call that shit out. In fact, we viciously dragged men *and* women in our own communities who tried to hold on to Bill Cosby and *The Cosby Show*. Black folks of a certain generation were hella resentful about being asked to give up watching such shows as an act of solidarity. For those of us born before 1990, the Huxtables were the first high-achieving, reasonably functional Black family that we got to see on TV. For most of the seasons during which it aired, it was a top-ranked sitcom. This meant that the Cosbys were a Black family that all Americans could relate to. I loved the Huxtables, particularly the youngest daughter, Rudy, who was near my age. But I gave them up, because after knowing of Bill Cosby's alleged crimes it was hard to watch him without remembering that I was watching a violent monster. *Black* women have been some of Bill Cosby's most vocal critics. We didn't just leave white women to fend for themselves. We came and got our people.

When evidence surfaced that actor Nate Parker and his writing partner and friend Jean Celestin were accused of running a train on a white woman without her consent when they were in college, Black feminists expressed outrage, boycotted Parker's ironically titled film, *The Birth of a Nation*, and demanded that he atone in a thoughtful way for any harm he might have caused this young woman, who eventually committed suicide. Parker and Celestin were both tried for sexual assault. Parker was acquitted while Celestin was initially found guilty. Later that verdict was thrown out. Parker maintained his innocence, but Black women, who are disproportionately victims of sexual assault, continued to empathize with the young woman and to hold Parker's and Celestin's feet to the fire. Black feminists were roundly blamed for the film being a flop in theaters. Still the position of Black feminists remains clear: first, do no harm.

No comparable outrage emerges from white feminists when Black women are under attack. Meanwhile, Black women pay a high price for our commitment to feminism in a culture that reveres our men, precisely because their extreme social vulnerability is on display. We are called divisive, man-hating, combative, unfeminine. All the usual shit. Those of us who are straight are often chastised for our outspokenness by being denied partnership. White feminists often struggle to even conceptualize Black female vulnerability, let alone to call out white men for harming Black women. When the various forms of structural challenges that Black women experience come to light, the response from white feminists is, more often than not, anemic.

White women and Black men share a kind of narcissism that comes from being viewed as the most vulnerable entities within their respective races. Black people hesitate to call out Black men for male privilege because they have experienced such devastation at the hands of a white supremacist system. And white women frequently don't recognize that though women are oppressed around the world, whiteness elevates the value of their femininity and allows them to get away with shit that women of color pay royally for.

Many Black men struggle to acknowledge that they experience male privilege. Some years ago, an internet writer published a Black male privilege checklist, modeled after Peggy McIntosh's white privilege checklist. Every time I have posted the Black male checklist, the level of bellyaching, backtracking, minimizing, and obscuring that Black men do is unmatched. Yes, it is true that Black men experience what famed Black feminist theorist Patricia Hill Collins has called a "subjugated masculinity." This means, like I discussed about Mann and Bob, that they are frustrated patriarchs. For instance, only male privilege could make

Barack Obama do the shit he did around My Brother's Keeper, a point I made previously. Only male privilege could eclipse the struggles of Black girls out of the view of a man who is a father to two daughters.

Perhaps the frustrated patriarch explanation can shed some light on why the Bill Cosby case is so appalling. His copious alleged sexual assaults of women play out a troubling script of a Black man obsessed with dominating and subjugating white women. There is racialized sexism at play in Bill Cosby's apparent choice of victims. The desire to violate predominantly white female victims at the height of the 1960s, when Cosby was one of the most powerful and visible Black male stars, suggests that, if these charges are true, his desire for power was tied uniquely to the ability to subjugate white women. There was a full one-hundred-year period between the end of slavery and the first allegations of Bill Cosby raping white women. That means there was a one-hundred-year period between the emergence of a narrative about dangerous Black male rapists and the instantiation of one who was serial in his brutality. For one hundred years, Black men had never *gotten away with it.* They were killed, mostly for rapes they didn't commit.

A history with those contours, a Black masculinity shaped in a toxic stew of white male rage and white-lady tears, might emerge with a perverted notion of freedom. Yes, it is true that the Cosby case is so extreme that it certainly does not reflect the everyday realities of most Black men. But most white people aren't members of the KKK, either. The most extreme versions of a pathology often have much to teach us about the less extreme forms those pathologies can take. If this were an episode of *Criminal Minds*, we could perhaps admit that if it is true that Cosby assaulted all these women, then white women became the target of his seething but sublimated Black male rage. The desire to dominate and humiliate white women is a logical extension of a racialized toxic masculinity, predicated on the idea that freedom is synonymous with white patriarchy. And white patriarchy inheres in both the dominating and the possessing of white women. Look, if it is true that Cosby committed even a portion of these crimes, it's not clear to me whether his hatred of white women was because he really wanted to be with one or because he simply despised what they had meant for the project of Black manhood. That kind of work is best left up to the psychoanalysts. What I know is that rape is about power, and if a Black man has been serially raping white women for nearly fifty years, this is a violent patriarchal form of hitting back at white supremacy.

In 1968, Black Panther Party leader Eldridge Cleaver wrote an infamous book called *Soul On Ice*, where he delved—scarily—into the psychosexual politics of Black men's relationships to white and Black women. He wrote, "The white man made the Black woman the symbol of slavery and the white woman the symbol of freedom. Every time I embrace a Black woman I'm embracing slavery, and when I put my arms around a white woman, well, I'm hugging freedom. . . . I will not be free until the day I can have a white woman in my bed and a white man minds his own business. Until that day comes, my entire existence is tainted, poisoned, and I will still be a slave—and so will the white woman." Thus, Cleaver concludes a few pages later, "I became a rapist." Infuriatingly, he recounts, "To refine my technique and *modus operandi*, I started out by practicing on black girls in the ghetto . . . and when I considered myself smooth enough, I crossed the tracks and sought out white prey." "Rape," Cleaver argues, "was an insurrectionary act. It delighted me that I was defying and trampling upon the white man's law, upon his system of values, and that I was defiling his women—and this point, I believe, was the most satisfying to me because I was very resentful over the historical fact of how the white man has used the black woman. I felt I was getting revenge." Does anyone else need a shower?

Now that you're back, let's talk about it. First, I know that many of you reading this are wondering what the fifty-year-old sexist ramblings of a racial madman have to do with racial and sexual attitudes today. Does the phrase "Make America Great Again" mean anything to you? So much of the racial animus that is shaping this current moment in American politics is a relitigation of the 1950s and 1960s. Often, in the polling data that shaped the Trump campaign, white Americans cited the 1950s as America's best decade. And perhaps the *Leave It To Beaver* years were really great—if you were white! The civil rights movement was not yet in full swing. The women's liberation movement had not yet begun. White men ruled, and white ladies looked pretty on TV. So going back to this moment is necessary to understand the kinds of racialized masculinity that white and Black men are negotiating in this moment. Also, far too often, we think history doesn't matter, but half the time that I spend with Black men talking about feminism makes me think I'm in some Black Power skit conjured up from 1973.

After reading Eldridge Cleaver's psychotic rambling, Bill Cosby's alleged crimes make far more sense. Both men became the self-fulfilling prophecies of white supremacy's worst lies about Black male sexuality. White folks needed monsters to justify their hatred, and white supremacy plus patriarchy created just the kind of primordial stew that could bring forth such creatures. We all have a political and ethical duty to reject the monsters white supremacy created, but we can't forget that white patriarchy itself is the biggest bang of them all. There is also a more hurtful truth that Eldridge Cleaver points us to in his frightening candor. He spoke of a deep-seated and collective hatred among Black men for Black women. White women represented freedom, while Black women represented slavery. Black women were the literal site for the reproduction of slavery.

Part of the reason no one delved fully into the racial politics of Cosby's alleged sex crimes is because they point us back to a key source of enmity between Black men and Black women, and Black women and white women—they force us to ask questions about interracial relationships that we would all rather shy away from speaking honestly about. But Ida B. Wells's critique of the sexual politics of racism shows us why interracial dating (between white and Black people) and interracial rape are conversations that intrinsically go together. Rape is tied to questions of power and consent, but interracial dating is tied to questions of power and freedom.

I believe wholeheartedly in the right of all consenting adults to choose the kinds of partnerships that are best for them, but I'm tired of the lie that relationships and love are not political. The struggle of queer folks to build families in the ways they desire demonstrate that love is political. I'm tired of the lie that desire is a pure social category, unhampered by the politics of race and gender.

Case in point: Jesse Williams, a biracial Black actor and one of the stars and heartthrobs of *Grey's Anatomy*, has a huge following among Black women. At the 2016 *BET Awards*, Williams gave a speech that went viral after he won the Humanitarian Award. He affirmed the Black Lives Matter movement, the many victims of police brutality, and the movement's largely female leadership. He also called out white cultural appropriation, saying, "We're done watching and waiting while this invention called 'whiteness' uses and abuses us, burying black people out of sight and out of mind while extracting our culture, our dollars, our entertainment like oil— black gold, ghettoizing and demeaning our creations then stealing them, gentrifying our genius and then trying us on like costumes before discarding our bodies like rinds of strange fruit." It was a perfect moment of a celebrity using his platform for good. I'm not even into light-skinned men, but in that moment, Jesse Williams was bae.

A few months later, Williams and his wife, whom he had saluted during the speech, announced they were divorcing. Much like having a Black wife had done wonders for Obama's credibility with Black America, Jesse Williams having a Black, regular-pretty, slightly thick and curvy wife also made Black women love him more. But when divorce reports surfaced, some tabloids suggested that Williams had been cheating with a white female costar. Though those news reports were never confirmed, the mere thought of it made Williams's stock go down quickly among Black women. The divorce we could understand. Marriage is hard. But the potential white girl—that was damn-near unforgivable. For once, Williams represented a Black man who had made it, who had great politics, and who had chosen a Black woman for a life partner. To most Black women, that choice matters.

Often when Black men show a vocal preference for white women, and Black women "feel some type of way about it," as millennials like to say, we are told that we are tripping over what is simply a matter of preference! My good friend Dr. Yaba Blay often says, "There is a thin line between preference and pathology." When Black men evince a preference for dating white women, solely or primarily, this crosses the line into the pathological. Conversely, there are Black men who have sophisticated structural analyses of white supremacy and of their oppressed conditions as Black men, but treat their intimate choices through a faulty color-blind lens in which Black women, in particular, are asked to view the whiteness of their choice of partner as merely incidental to a larger narrative of love that transcends racial boundaries. This is bullshit.

I'm tired of Black men who are race men everywhere but in the bedroom. I'm tired of Black men who buy into the lie that their choice of white female partners shouldn't concern anyone but them. That thinking is ahistorical. Courtesy of white supremacy, Black women have always had to care whom Black men were dating. Black and white people have never had the luxury of apolitical romance. Yet, when Black women give either the overt or internal eye roll to the polished (seemingly), got-it-together brother walking down the street with the white chick on his arm, we are cast as bitter and angry. Maybe we should just start admitting that we *are* angry at seeing some of our best and brightest brothers choose white women for partners. There. I said it. Because it is we, Black women, who labor under the historical narrative of having our bodies cast as the unique and singular site for unfreedom. That's a heavy load to bear in a country that romanticizes freedom and justice for all. Of course, we are resentful of brothers whose freedom dreams are personified by the ability to date and fuck white women with ease.

I'm tired of meeting white women with no race analysis who marry Black men and make these men feel like their race—their Blackness—is not a primary thing that defines them. For many Black men, the best-case scenario is that they can create a part of their lives where they are not solely defined by Black manhood. The worst-case scenario is that they think white womanhood is some kind of come-up from the abjection of Black womanhood.

This is why I don't have any problem with Black women who choose to partner with people who are not Black. The logic of reverse racism won't work here, for any of you who were planning on trying it. In the chapter "Love in a Hopeless Place," I lay out the challenges that Black girls face in trying to find partners. There is a real numbers problem that Black women confront, even though they are the least likely to marry someone who isn't Black. This kind of racial loyalty often circumscribes Black women's intimate options in ways that cause us to be alone forever. Moreover, if dating-site statistics are to be believed, Black women are the least likely of any demographic (Latina and Asian women, white, Black, Latino, and Asian men) to receive responses to their dating profiles. This cultural and intimate hatred of Black women is a feminist issue, one that all feminists, Black and non-Black alike, should care about.

In Kate Weigand's book *Red Feminism*, she tells a fascinating story about Black women who participated in the Communist Party (CP) in the 1930s. In 1934, Black women organizers asked the Party leadership to outlaw interracial marriages among members. Many of the Black men had married or begun dating white women, but white men weren't showing comparable interest in dating or marrying Black women. The Party's leadership appointed Abner Berry, a Black party leader who was married to a white woman, to deal with the crisis. In typical Black-man fashion, he called Black women's demands to outlaw interracial marriage "counterrevolutionary." But he did institute organizing sessions on the triple oppressions of race, class, and gender that Black women faced. Apparently, the party members also tried to teach white male communists how to dance so they would be more comfortable approaching Black women at parties.

These are not new problems. In many ways, prospects in heterosexual dating are far more dismal today than they were eighty years ago. But in the 1930s, radical left organizers framed Black women's limited intimate options as a structural problem. They didn't fall into the neoliberal trap of framing everything as a simple matter of individual choice. They also seemed to understand that if they were going to use Black women's labor to build movements for social change, they had a responsibility to care about the quality of Black women's personal lives. We have far less clarity today about the ways that Black women's intimate lives, whether they are in straight or queer partnerships, should be a part of our political frameworks.

I absolutely know that love doesn't adhere to racial lines. (Even I have a *white-boys-who-could-get-it* list.) But the choice of whom to love is political. And if white feminists were honest, they would recognize that their feminism actually does demand that they interrogate the political dimensions of their intimate engagements. Those white women married to white men overwhelmingly expressed their solidarity with Donald Trump, clearly placing racial solidarity and agreement with white supremacy over any kind of gender solidarity. Those white women who have partnered with Black men must reckon with what that choice means, in light of histories where white women are cast as the stuff of which racial freedom dreams are made. White women and, specifically, white feminists have to reckon with their complicity and often full participation in this set of social narratives about Black sexuality that has been exceedingly dangerous to the well-being of Black lives.

A woke white feminism would recognize that even as they rebel against the sexual strictures of white patriarchy, through movements to reclaim the term "slut" and so forth, they have a duty to recognize that white men's desires to regulate their sexual lives is predicated not just on controlling white women's bodies, but also on criminalizing Black men and denigrating Black women. The movement to defund Planned Parenthood, an organization that provides critical health care to many poor women of color, has nothing to do with the desire of white men on the right for Black and Latina women to have more babies. Rather, these men seek to control reproduction itself because they want to control the life possibilities of all women. So much of right-leaning social policy in the 1980s and 1990s was predicated on white men controlling white women's bodies by uplifting the purity and sanctity of white femininity and simultaneously maligning Black womanhood and Black femininity.

I've already mentioned the way the term "welfare queens" has been used on the right to summarily vilify Black women. But the idea of the "welfare queen" is itself a myth, created for nefarious purposes. In 1976, Ronald Reagan began telling stories about a completely fabricated group of system abusers that he called "welfare queens." He named a nonexistent social phenomenon based on a singular incident of abuse of welfare benefits by one woman in Chicago in the 1970s. But white people who resented the racial and class progress of the 1960s found a convenient target in hating allegedly undeserving Black women, who all got subsumed under the category of welfare queens. From the first time he deployed the term in his 1976 presidential campaign, until 1996, when Bill Clinton passed his infamous welfare reform bill, white male politicians on both the right and the semi-left used cultural enmity toward Black women to mobilize a conservative backlash against the 1960s.

A decade later, two cases cemented the enduring power of the Black male rapist myth from one hundred years earlier. In 1986, William Horton, a prisoner who was serving a life sentence for robbery and murder in Massachusetts, was allowed to participate in a weekend prison furlough program. He failed to return, and ten months later raped and beat a white woman from suburban Maryland while her husband was bound and gagged and forced to listen. During the 1988 presidential race, the George H. W. Bush campaign ran incendiary television ads that conveniently renamed William Horton "Willie Horton" and cast him as a monster that liberal Michael Dukakis, the Democratic nominee, had let out of jail.

A year later, a white woman was brutally raped and beaten in Central Park, and five young Black and Latino men were arrested for the crime. After more than a decade in jail, all five young men were exonerated by DNA evidence. Donald Trump took out a full-page ad in 1989 in several New York newspapers, including *The New York Times*, calling for New York to bring back the death penalty so these young men could be executed. In 2014, he called the $41 million settlement the five men were awarded "the heist of the century." One month before he was elected president, he doubled down in a CNN interview, saying that the young men had all "admitted they were guilty." They were teenagers at the time, and their testimony had been coerced. Moreover, DNA evidence correctly identified the actual perpetrator of the crime back in 2002. In the interim years between their arrest and the overturning of their convictions, the presumed guilt of the Central Park Five contributed to a powerful narrative exploited by politicians on the right and the left, everyone from Reagan to Bush I to Bill Clinton about the need to "get tough on crime" and put away "Black male superpredators," whom the Clintons (both Bill and Hillary) argued began terrorizing communities at as early as thirteen years of age.

With his 1994 crime bill and his 1996 welfare reform

package, Clinton, with the help of a Republican Congress, sounded a late-twentieth-century death knell for Black social progress, all rooted in an insidious narrative about the danger of Black sexuality—it turned Black men into rapists and Black women into baby machines. In this narrative, white women were everything Black women were not—socially responsible, well-behaved, marriageable. Therefore, they were the kind of women that Black men should desire but of which they should never ever understand themselves to be worthy.

The obsession with curtailing reproductive freedom in this country is about forcing white women to be hyperproductive in service of reproducing a white Republic. As of 2014, most children born in the United States are not white. This important demographic shift has only heightened anxiety about declining birth rates among white families. God, the right would have us believe, wants America to remain white. The only way that can happen is for heterosexual white people to keep getting married and reproducing.

When Ida B. Wells gave the written side eye to the white-girl tears of her day, she was hoping that maybe by doing so, those folks listening could attune their ear to the fervent cries of Black women being raped by white men all over the country. But Wells learned something that every Black girl learns at some point. When white girls cry, every other girl's tears cease to matter. However, what the Trump era has come to teach white women is that uncritical solidarity with patriarchy is tantamount to sticking your head in a lion's mouth. Too many white women thought they could vote for Trump while sticking everyone else with the consequences. In the battle over power, when white men run the world, white-lady tears have diminishing returns. This fact alone should inspire an army of white feminists to arm themselves with boxes of Kleenex, march into the world of white women, and start doing the painful work of trying to change their sisters' minds.

NEVER SCARED

In the summer of 2008, *The New Yorker* featured a cover called "The Politics of Fear." The cover depicted an Afro-wearing, gun-toting Michelle Obama and her husband, presidential candidate Barack Obama, clad in a turban, in the Oval Office, engaging in a conspiratorial fist bump under a picture of Osama Bin Laden. Created by Barry Blitt, the cover, according to the magazine, sought to "satirize the use of scare tactics and misinformation in the presidential election to derail Barack Obama's campaign." Americans on the right expressed angst about whether Michelle Obama was a militant Angry Black Woman and whether her husband, whose father had been Muslim, was himself a sympathizer with those who erroneously used Islam to justify terroristic acts. The cover was roundly condemned. Blitt had gambled that coming face-to-face with their ugliest and most entrenched ideas about the Obamas, about Black men and women, and about Muslims would force American conservatives to realize the absurdity of these belief systems. It did not. The cover seemed to reinscribe rather than to resist the stereotypes, since it trusted that white Americans would be able to acknowledge their own problematic assumptions about race.

In 2015, at her Tuskegee University commencement speech, Mrs. Obama responded specifically to this cover, which she argued was rooted in the "fears and misperceptions of others." Those fears and misperceptions brought up questions about her, such as "Was I too loud, or too angry or too emasculating?" She said that the cover "knocked [her] back a bit," and made her wonder "just how are others seeing me?" The anti-Blackness at the heart of white fear is predicated on a misrecognition of the humanity of Black people. Whether that misrecognition is willful or unwitting matters less than its harmful outcomes. Impact matters more than intent.

Donald Trump is the logical extension of white America's most fantastical and distorted ideas about people of color and their power in the Americas. Despite Barack Obama's eventual wins in 2008 and 2012, the fear that Blitt captured in his cover presaged a rise of populist resentment against the Obamas specifically, and Blacks and Muslims in general, that would come roaring back fiercely. In the 2016 elections, white fear ruled the day. Trump used fear to prime the pumps of white American racial resentment by fanning the flames of the birther myth against Barack Obama, claiming that Obama was not a native-born American citizen. For years Trump stoked the fires of the birther myth, continuing even after Canadian-born Ted Cruz became his primary opposition in the 2016 Republican primaries. Donald Trump deftly used the narrative of national belonging to make some groups, namely white male voters (across class lines), feel visible, heard, and affirmed. All voters should have access to candidates that make them feel recognized, but there's a problem when your notion of recognition is predicated on someone else's exclusion. There's a problem when visibility becomes a zero-sum game, where making one group's demands visible renders every other group's political concerns obscure. Only white supremacy demands such exacting and fatalistic math.

Trying to make sense of the 2016 election outcome, Toni Morrison named the problem one of white fear. "The sad plight of grown white men, crouching beneath their (better) selves, to slaughter the innocent during traffic stops, to push black women's faces into the dirt, to handcuff black children. Only the frightened would do that. Right?" she inquires of us. "So scary are the consequences of a collapse of white privilege that many Americans have flocked to a political platform that supports and translates violence against the defenseless as strength. These people are not so much angry as terrified, with the kind of terror that makes knees tremble."

I once read that the root of all anger is fear, particularly a fear of those things we cannot control. White rage is deeply connected to a fear of losing privilege and status in a browning American empire. When your entire worldview is predicated on being on top, sinking from the top even a little bit can feel like an annihilation. My fluffy friends, those who have had many more years of therapy than I have had, are quick to tell me that feelings and emotions are not to be judged and that there are no right and wrong feelings. Feelings just *are*. But I am as judgmental as I can possibly be of white fear. It is an illegitimate political emotion that has done no good that I can think of, and more harm than it is humanly possible to tally. To say it in terms that the "all lives matter" crowd might understand, all fears matter, but some fears are treated as though they matter more.

To be Black is to grow up in a world where white feelings can become dangerous weapons. If you're Black, white fear is frequently lethal. I'm willing to concede my skepticism toward feelings as a potential personality flaw, but my approach to life is to view feelings as employees that can't be trusted—which is to say, my feelings are subject to intense micromanagement. I have to be clear about how I want my feelings to work for me. I set up strict parameters and rules about how they should be engaged, the lines they can't cross, and I am quick to put my feelings in a time out when I feel they are getting out of hand. Frankly, I resent others who allow their feelings to roam around unmanaged, demanding everybody's attention.

My feelings, for their part, go on strike against me all the time, showing up with picket signs that scream truths I'd rather not hear, all while demanding that I renegotiate terms. But if you are Black and hope to live to adulthood, micromanaging your feelings is necessary for survival. Your feelings can't go on strike in the workplace. You can't karate chop every white retail service person who follows you around a store, is rude to you on the phone, or takes their good sweet time bringing your food to the table. You also can't karate chop the well-meaning white friend who moves to reassure you that "it wasn't racial. Clearly they're just jerks."

I think I am a micromanager of feelings because my

Black mama didn't play that. Pouting, angry tears, and back talk were strictly not allowed in our house. The image of children stomping up the stairs and slamming doors after getting mad at their parents was some shit reserved for white families on TV. I was convinced as a child that if I ever tried such a thing in my mother's house, she already had a burial site picked out for me. Always sensitive and quick to cry after being scolded, I tried mightily to hold back tears lest I hear my mother saying, "Suck up all that crying before I really give you something to cry about." Unlike many Black children in my community, my mother wasn't fond of giving whippings. Those were few and far between for me. But the specter of the switch or the belt was always there—for me and for every Black kid I knew. That was what my community understood good parenting to be. Unmanaged emotions were one swift way to arrange a summit for your rear end and the belt. No one had time for my intense Black-girl emotions.

Black children learn early that our fears are not, and cannot be, the first order of business in a family trying to survive. When I was seven, and starting the third grade, my mother asked me one day, "If I get you a key to the house, do you feel like you can come home on the bus after school every day and stay by yourself until I get home from work?" "No," I told her, "I would just like to keep going to daycare." The look on my mom's face, a mix of disappointment, distress, and a bit of disdain, told me that "No" had not been the right answer. It wasn't really a question.

Skyrocketing childcare costs continue to disadvantage Black families, particularly in households like mine, headed by a single breadwinner mother. According to the Institute for

Women's Policy Research, 60.9 percent of all Black families are headed by a single mother who is the breadwinner for the family. Another 20 percent of Black households rely on a married mother as the breadwinner. In every state in the United States, there are more single than married Black mothers. In every state in the United States, there are more married white mothers than single ones. In twenty-four states, the cost of childcare exceeds the cost of rent, and in many states the cost of childcare exceeds the 10 percent income-affordability threshold established by federal agencies. In my hometown, childcare currently costs 8 percent of a family's budget, that is, if they make enough to meet cost-of-living standards. And if you live in a big city, forget about it. In the 1980s, my mother was an hourly employee for a local construction firm. Childcare costs surely exceeded the affordability threshold.

At age seven, my latchkey status became official. I was just going to have to "be a big girl," get over my fear of monsters in the closet and boogie men under the bed, and do my mama a solid. To manage both our fears, my mother insisted that I call her as soon as I walked into the house and closed and locked the door behind me. I was not allowed to go outside until she came home. And when darkness came earlier and earlier at the end of each fall, I would turn on all the lights, walk into all the rooms, and make sure no one who shouldn't be there was there. I don't know if latchkey adulthood is a thing, but since I have lived alone for the entirety of my adult life, I do often still turn on all the lights when I arrive home and walk into all the rooms to make sure there are no intruders. Part of what being a latchkey kid taught me is that overcoming fear is first and foremost about having the courage to look under the bed.

Black girls learn that managing our fears is the key to our families' ability to survive and thrive. At the beginning of third grade, I conquered my fear of being home alone for the greater good of my family. By the beginning of fourth grade, my mother had saved enough even on her limited income to purchase a modest ranch-style home for the two of us. She didn't tell me then, but perhaps this was the plan all along. Either her money could go to childcare, or it could go toward an investment in our future. Nearly thirty years after my mother was making these kinds of choices, working moms of color too often still have to choose between housing security and child care. In order for my mother's plan to work, I had to do my seven-year-old-Black-girl part and refuse to let whatever boogie monsters were under my bed not have the final say. What might it mean to start from the perspective of a Black girl's fears and build a world that is safe for her? In hindsight, I can see the material difference it made when I agreed with my mom that I was "big girl" enough to stay home. No matter who you are, the stakes of giving in to your fears are high.

One of my Sunday school teachers told us that F.E.A.R.s are just "fantasies, expecting a reality." Years later, a different teacher told us that fears are just "false expectations appearing real." Black Christianity demands that we regularly confront our fears and identify the falsities that shape them. From childhood forward, you are told to memorize the words of 2 Timothy 1:7: "God has not given us a spirit of fear, but of power, and of love, and of a sound mind." This verse was to be kept in the spiritual arsenal for moments when anxiety and fear began to encroach on your sense of peace. When you felt anxious, you were supposed to speak back to your fears, reminding them that fear does not come from a divine place. We were learning that our fears, like our feelings in general, were not facts. No matter the clever acronym, fear was rooted in falsity and fantasy. Fear was always a thing to be managed by increasing our faith.

In fact, I do believe fear and faith can coexist. But what I appreciate is that the Black Church demands a continual reckoning with what is true and what is false. Often religious traditions, invested as they are in what many think of as the mythic and fantastical, are not given credit for being invested in anything real. But the Black Church is one of the historic structuring institutions for the social life of Black people, and it has always known that part of Black survival is about having the best tools to assess what is and is not a real threat. In other words, the Black Church doesn't have the luxury of acting like white supremacy, sexism, and homophobia aren't real. These structural forces take Black lives every day, sometimes through violent deaths, sometimes after a lifetime of privation. Because of the commitment of Black churches to running food pantries and tax workshops for the elderly and trying to meet the needs of impoverished folks in their local communities, they know well that some of the material realities Black people face are scary. As I said in the "Grown Woman Theology" chapter, churches have an exceedingly long way to go in combating matters of homophobia and sexism. And, frankly, modern-day Black churches also have to reckon with all the ways in which they have walked away from the clarity of King's generation about the role the church should play in ending white supremacy. Still, it was at church that I learned how to have a healthy relationship with my fears, anxieties, and fantasies.

White fear is not subject to any such cultural or religious scrutiny. In fact, white fears are routinely treated as fact rather than fantasy. When the police shot John Crawford in August 2014 in a Walmart in Beavercreek, Ohio, those who called 911 said he was walking around the store pointing the gun at people. Later the man who made that call retracted his statement, but his retraction came too late. Video footage confirms that John Crawford simply perched the air rifle, which he had picked up at the store, on his shoulder as he shopped. In this instance, white fear of the fantastical threat of Black men caused the police to take John Crawford's life. Three months later, two police officers rolled up on and shot Tamir Rice, a twelve-year-old kid playing with a toy gun in a park near his neighborhood. The cops who shot Tamir without even giving him a chance to put down the gun or identify it as a toy claimed to have feared for their lives. None of these officers was charged and convicted; their fears were treated as facts. In other words, white fears rest on the presumption that they are rooted in fact; everyone who is nonwhite is treated as though their fears are the stuff of fantasy.

In April 2017, a Texas police officer shot and killed fifteen-year-old Jordan Edwards as he and his brothers were frantically driving away from a party where other young people had started shooting. That officer, Roy Oliver, was fired and charged with murder. He subsequently pled not guilty. But Jordan Edwards is still dead. Fear—over having your life or a loved one's life snatched away by those sworn to protect and serve—is at least one of the emotions that animates the cry of "Black Lives Matter." Most white people fixate on the anger and rage that feels palpable at Black Lives Matter protests. They view this rage with a studied indifference and a willful ignorance that is about not seeing or validating Black people's fear and right to be afraid. In the era of Fox News and fake news, the Black Lives Matter movement has been branded a "hate group" on par with the Ku Klux Klan. One online interlocutor characterized the political program of BLM as a desire for "Black supremacy." Black supremacy is not a thing, if you were wondering. But the same folks who believe in the possibility of Black supremacy also have a problem with Black Entertainment Television, Black History Month, and T-shirts that proclaim that Black Girls Rock. I refuse to spend my time trying to help these kinds of basic-ass white people.

White fear is the cultural refuse of white supremacy. Strewn about and never properly disposed of, it becomes an environmental hazard for those of us who must live in the neighborhoods (metaphoric and otherwise) where white folks choose to dump all their shit. If I'm being generous (and I'm not required to be generous), I can understand why shifting power relations in a world where white folks have always been unequivocally dominant could have them all in their feelings. The problem is that, with the exception of former president Barack Obama and a few well-placed Black millionaires and billionaires, *Black people don't have any appreciable levels of institutional power.* The U.S. Senate currently has three Black senators. That's the most it's ever had, and we are nearly two decades into the twenty-first century. In 2013, the median net wealth for white families was over $141,000. For Black families, it was $11,000. According to a joint study by the Institute for Policy Studies and the Corporation for Enterprise Development, it would take Black people 228 years to catch up to the amount of net wealth that white people currently possess. White people fear a fantastical rise of racial power that they have made damn-near structurally impossible for Black people to achieve.

Letting fear rule is dangerous if you're a regular person. If you have levels of privilege and power unmatched in the modern world, being ruled by fear is catastrophic for those with less power than you. Fear of Black people is one of the grandest delusions of white supremacy. It's the reason why even police officers of color—Black, Asian, and Latino—are often quick on the trigger when they are policing Black men. In Charlotte, North Carolina, on September 20, 2016, a Black officer shot Keith Lamont Scott as he was sitting in his car waiting on his grandchild to get off the school bus. The officer said Scott looked suspicious and that he feared for his life. Scott had no weapon. A Latino officer shot Philando Castile. White fear of Black people is not limited to white Americans. It is rooted in the ideology of white supremacy, a virus that infects us all. That Black lives are at the mercy of those emboldened and sanctioned by the state to enact the worst of their fantasies upon us is enough to make us lose faith in the whole damn system.

Curiosity is often the first casualty of the politics of fear. Sometimes the things we fear most are our questions. More specifically, we fear the questions to which we don't have answers. When we are afraid, we stop asking questions and start seeking short-term solutions. The work of my hands is the work of teaching students how to ask more and better questions. It is the work of rescuing curiosity from the clutches of fear. What kind of world can (white) fear really create? What is the end game of white supremacy? And what would it mean to start from the fears of the marginalized and build a world that is safe for them?

Though I grew up in a religious household, my mother and stepfather encouraged my questions. But I was so obsessed with getting the right answer that often my natural skepticism took a back seat to my overachiever impulses. Having a carefully ordered world is important for working-class Black girls trying to make it out of the neighborhood and on to bigger and better. And sometimes the hood and the structures that beget it don't make time for Black kids with questions. At some point, it became more important to me to pass the tests, get the right SAT scores, write perfect literary analyses of novels, and produce scholarship-winning essays for college than to nurture my endless curiosity.

It was years of extended access to the classroom that helped me overcome my fear of asking questions. If we cannot or will not ask questions, then we are far, far from the path to freedom. Orderly knowledge systems appeal to that part of me that is always seeking a clear and linear path forward. But, of course, life is not given to linearity. I already told y'all that I'm a micromanager of emotions, and sometimes our questions show up in the form of feelings. Part of learning to manage our feelings is learning to confront our questions.

One way that we've seen questions arrive in the form of

feelings is in the generalized white anxiety and distrust of President Obama. Rather than digging deep to find the question at the core of the anxiety, too many white people let the feeling become an indicator of Obama's fitness and right to lead. The question—"Can I, a white person, trust a Black man to lead this country?"—was left unasked by too many. There are also liberal white folks who went into the voting booth believing they could. But they stopped after asking the question one time. Voting once or even twice for a Black man is not enough to undo years of anti-Black social conditioning. Fear and feelings, especially about racism, have to be managed constantly. White supremacy does not fall through singular acts of white resistance and magnanimity. There are assuredly people who voted for Obama in 2008 and then voted for Trump in 2016. This is because their support for Obama was predicated on him emerging as some sort of Magical Black Jesus figure. When he couldn't meet such ridiculous expectations, many white folks returned to their comfort zone.

Every time I write about the emotional lives of white people, some white person sends me an email or a tweet and tells me, "How dare you act like you know what white folks are thinking?!" Haven't white folks learned that Black folks know them far better than they know themselves? Our survival is predicated on our willingness to study you, your impulses, your hard expressions, your laughter (and whether it reaches your eyes), your gifts, and your lies. Black survival means being endlessly obsessed with figuring out the depths to which white folks will fall to maintain a position of dominance. Sometimes Black survival requires that we be the wet nurses and handmaidens for an endless project of white navel-gazing. In order to save our own lives, we have to be brutally honest about what the worst of white folks, as Kiese Laymon calls them, are capable of, even if no one else will.

Politicians on the right know that the kind of work we do in college classrooms—the work of inquiry and deep questioning, the work of nurturing curiosity, the work of exposing the myths and fantasies that inform students' fears—can create an informed and powerful citizenry. The students who sit in college classrooms like mine today can become powerful leaders in the fight against racism, sexism, and homophobia two decades from now. Politicians seek to quash all possibility of this kind of work. Recently I found out that I had been placed on a "professor watchlist" for a national nonprofit organization whose mission is to remove "liberal bias" from the college classroom. What they mean by "liberal bias" is that they don't want a Black woman standing in a classroom, teaching college students that racism is real, sexism is a problem, homophobia is repugnant, and capitalism and the elitism it begets are worthy of our deepest skepticism. This is not knowledge, they say. It's my "racial agenda" governing how I run my classroom. By letting me know that they are watching me, they are hoping to scare me. But this is why I'm "never scared," as we say in the crunk South. This doesn't mean I'm never afraid. Being never scared has a cultural inflection to it that is about defiance, and about a refusal to be cowed into submission. To be black is to know you are being watched—at all times—anyway.

This is, in fact, the conundrum of being a Black woman in the academy; that we are simultaneously hypervisible and

invisible. Patricia Hill Collins once called the constant surveillance that attends to our movement in the ivory tower
the politics of containment. Being under the presence of the
white gaze is supposed to elicit different behavior from me—
namely to curtail whatever illicit behaviors that I am automatically presumed to be engaging in. Moving through the
world as though under the constant gaze of white folks is
something Black people with middle-class aspirations are
taught from a young age to perfect. To repeat part two of the
Respectables' Credo: "Never let them catch you slippin'."
Be perfect. Never fuck up.

And my response is, "Fuck all that." Sometimes you
have to have the clarity that Ida B. Wells had when she told
white people the truth about themselves and their lynching
lies. She knew she was poking the hornet's nest, but it was a
"Give me liberty or give me death" moment. Now, look. Any
given day in my college classroom is never that dramatic.
Mostly I don't go in thinking my life is on the line. But with
the uptick in open-carry permits on college campuses, and
white men's penchant for taking out their anger, frustra-
tion, entitlement, and anxiety on innocent bystanders, the
stakes of telling the truth are becoming higher and higher.
Right-wing organizations are not above using threats and
intimidation to corral and suffocate modes of knowledge
production that challenge the politics of fear. They insist
that I be scared. But what they don't know is that I've been
slaying boogie men since age seven. White folks are not entitled to my fear.

When I was in graduate school, it was customary that when
Black students ran into each other on our predominantly

white Southern campus, we would stop, embrace, and chat it up, so happy were we to see other friendly Black faces in what could sometimes be a hostile environment. But, frequently, if there were more than three of us together, white faculty or students might walk by and passive-aggressively say, "Oh what are y'all over here doing? Plotting the revolution?" Our running joke whenever more than three of us were gathered was to yell, "Disperse, disperse! You know they can't handle it." The joke was that we kept right on talking, out in the open, even though we knew we were conspicuous. It was our way of giving a middle finger to our very real fear of institutional surveillance and containment.

There is something deeply profane about the politics of white fear and, for this reason, the sacred is not the only register in which Black folks should respond to it. Because fear is an emotion viscerally experienced in the body, Black expressive culture that engages the body is one of the places where we work out shit that we can't make sense of any other way. Southern booty-shake music, the kind of stuff you can twerk to, is the place where I find the most productive synergy between the sacred and the profane, the place where I feel the most bodily freedom to let all my emotions—particularly the uncomfortable ones like anger and fear—hang out and find free expression. In both the Blues and Southern Hip Hop, Black folks have explicitly thrown off the vestiges of respectability politics to say the shit that needs to be said. But I'm a child of Hip Hop, not the Blues, and when I need to work out my feelings in a bodily fashion, it is to Hip Hop that I turn, to *Crunk* to be exact.

Crunk music, that brand of Hip Hop indigenous to Atlanta,

and to the South more generally, gives me the lyrical and bodily vocabulary to stand up to our collective cultural bullies with my middle fingers up. Whether it's the Young-bloodz yelling, "If you don't give a damn, we don't give a FUCK!" or Bone Crusher reminding his foes that he "ain't never scared," crunkness has always been the soundtrack to my resistance. It has kept me supplied in the lyrical defiance necessary to look white supremacy in the face and emerge victorious.

Rejecting the politics of fear is a primary sensibility if you were born into the Age of Hip Hop. This has been true ever since rap group N.W.A became famous and targeted for their song "Fuck Tha Police." Defiant and unafraid, these young men rapped about being regular victims of police ha-rassment and brutality and they rejected the politics of def-erence that many police feel is compulsory. Refusing to be nice to an officer, especially when he pulls you over on a lu-dicrous charge is not, in fact, against the law. Incivility is not illegal. The police know that, which is why they are jerks to Black citizens on the regular. I was only seven years old when N.W.A told the police exactly what they thought of them; thus, I was a little young to need or resonate with their defiant sensibility. Nearly thirty years after N.W.A became our gen-erational prophets of Black rage, these same rage-inducing conditions persist.

This is why grown-ass Black women need Beyoncé. With me, it always comes back to Beyoncé. While her pop an-thems gave me all the feminist good feelings in my twenties, Grown Woman Beyoncé, the Beyoncé that has emerged since her 2013 eponymous album, is on something different.

Like I mentioned before, Black feminists had all the feelings about Bey telling bitches to "bow down" on her song "Flawless." But every time I think about this Trump presidency, about the magnitude of the destruction it is heaping on communities of color, I'm grateful for every angry anthem Bey ever made. This kind of give-no-fucks anthem has been put here for such a prophetic time as this—a time in which white supremacists feel bold enough to try it. And because my personal mantra has long been "Be unapologetic," I can be found on any given day twerking (or trying my damnedest to twerk) to "I Ain't Sorry," one of my favorite tracks on her blockbuster visual album *Lemonade.*

"Formation," the debut track on *Lemonade,* is an invitation to a Black-girl conjuring session. In the song, the High Priestess of Hip Hop Culture tells us, "Okay ladies. Now, let's get in formation." She is calling us into very particular formations—the kinds of collective gatherings that can shift the culture, that can combat white supremacy, and sexism, and homophobia, the kinds of spaces that can use Black-girl magic to change the world. When Beyoncé tells all the fly chicks to get in formation, she is asking us to get our shit together so we can do the work that needs to be done. And the stakes are high as hell, because Black people are being killed. So, she reminds us, "Slay, trick. Or you get eliminated." Now that might be a reference to some kind of dance competition. But it's also a revision of "Never let them catch you slippin'." Be the best. Be exceptional. Or get eliminated.

The video for "Formation" pays homage to post-Katrina New Orleans and ends with Bey using the weight of her body to sink a New Orleans police cruiser into the flood's waters. Putting middle fingers up to the state that incarcerates the most people per capita anywhere on the globe, and including an image of a Black boy dancing for his life while staring down a line of police in riot gear, is a bold fuck-you to the forces that seek to snuff out Black lives. I fucks with Grown Woman Beyoncé, even more than I fucked with her during my girlhood, because *Lemonade* gives us a portrait of a Black woman reckoning with her rage, in both its intimate and its structural dimensions.

But I also love the political vision that emerges from the visual album that accompanies *Lemonade*. That political vision centers its hope in the collective magic, the indefatigable stamina, and the enduring power of Black women and girls. When Beyoncé used her own body to sink that police cruiser, she reminded us of all the ways Black women are willing to put their lives on the line to combat state violence. The sacrifices that Black women and girls make create more opportunities and possibilities for our communities. Getting into formation with other like-minded folks is one way we can help our fears not to win. In those formations, we can find joy, support, and strategies to help us overcome. When Black girls get in formation, the nation should follow.

LOVE IN A HOPELESS PLACE

My grandmother had this way of beginning conversations with me in the middle. Perhaps you figured that out from the impromptu sex talk. She'd start conversations with an accusation. On the regular, she told me, "You need to stop being so mean! Then you could get a boyfriend!" After saying this, she'd cut her roaming eyes at me, scolding, assessing, and *reading* me. It was as though she had been waiting on an opportunity to tell me about myself. *Who says my goal in life is to get a boyfriend, Grandmama?! And if by "mean," you mean "serious," about my business, and inhospitable to bullshit, well, wonder where I got that from?!* Fuming internally, I just shook my head, frustrated at this unsolicited intrusion and unwelcome advice. How could I tell Grandmama that my lack of a boyfriend wasn't because of a lack of desire on my part? From what I could ascertain, absolutely nobody wanted me. She started these conversations with me during my vacations home from college, which was just about the same time I realized that education and smarts weren't necessarily a pathway to finding a bae.

My grandmama had never understood why I wanted to go thousands of miles away, "upstate" as Southerners call it, to college. "Stop studyin' yourself!" she'd admonish every time she caught seven- or eight-year-old me zoned out in a world of my own thoughts. "All those books gone run ya crazy," she'd pronounce emphatically. Maybe she was right. My love for books had taken me miles and miles away. To the world of beautiful Black boys at Howard. I wasn't the first in my family to attend college, but my goal was to be the first to graduate. That meant I had to keep my head in the books and my legs closed. Neither my mother nor my grandmother ever preached such a sermon to me. But they didn't have to. Ambition was its own motivation. I couldn't let knuckleheaded boys come along and ruin my life chances. At least, this is what I told myself. But staying in the books and then later focusing on my career wasn't in the least bit hard when literally no one was trying to date me.

How could I tell my grandmother that? That I didn't have half the swag she'd apparently had at my age. That brothers didn't want me. And that it wasn't a figment of my imagination. On two separate occasions at Howard, first with King and then with Rob, classmates had looked me in my face and said, "You're so unattractive." I had dared on both occasions to beat each of them in an argument. When they were left without anything of substance to say, they both did what men learn to do when they can't dominate a woman intellectually—they berate her physically. But I wasn't a feminist yet. I didn't know then that this is one way patriarchy shows up. I cried in front of Rob, despite myself, which only made him despise me more. By the time it happened with King, I was less taken aback. Still, I had been humiliated by two men who figured out the easiest way to rob me of my sense of victory. They made me feel unlovable.

I hadn't wanted either of them and had cared little about their romantic assessments of me. Still, I winced upon learning that being smart had made me ugly to them. They were willing to say it, but I wondered what other romantic suitors had come to similar conclusions. Just how undesirable was I? Maybe this is why college had been a romantic drought for me. Maybe I was what the Combahee River Collective called smart-ugly: "We discovered that all of us, because we were 'smart' had also been considered 'ugly,' i.e., 'smart-ugly.' 'Smart-ugly' crystallized the way in which most of us had been forced to develop our intellects at great cost to our 'social' lives. The sanctions in the Black and white communities against Black women thinkers is comparatively much higher than for white women, particularly ones from the educated middle and upper classes." The women of Combahee put a language to the way that patriarchy and the men who love it separate women into categories of smart and pretty. Or friendable and fuckable. The girls who manage to be the perfect combination of both have access to some juju that I still haven't figured out.

On another occasion, a guy friend asked me one night while we were working on a campus project, "Brittney, why don't you have a boyfriend?" He had a girlfriend, so I knew this wasn't some awkward roundabout attempt of his to kick it to me. I sat, searching for an answer but coming up with none. Really, I wanted to reply, "I don't know. Can you tell me why?" It was an odd question, one that I didn't have an answer for then, one that I don't have an answer for now. That question haunted me, for the rest of college, for the entirety of my twenties, and for a good portion of my thirties.

What *is* wrong with me?

My grandmother said I was too mean, but surely some of my overly serious demeanor was a mask, an armor designed to keep men from seeing my innermost feelings. How could I take off the armor when there were no guarantees that men would recognize and, more to the point, *want* the real me? And what was wrong with being a woman who preferred the company of her own thoughts much of the time? On plenty of occasions, men, white and Black alike, have yelled at me to "Smile!" when they catch me going about my day zoned off in my own world. Grandmama had tried to warn me from childhood that "studyin' myself" would cause trouble. But I didn't listen, never making the connection that such practices made me seem like the stereotype—angry and unapproachable. It mattered less that white folks think unsmiling Black women are plotting the revolution. I revel in denying them smiles. But it felt costly to know that brothers were using similar assessments—that women who weren't smiling were women who had no interest in romance. *Simpletons.* Or, as we might call such brothers today, *basics*.

Grandmama began sounding the alarm about my singleness long before the rest of the family did. But when I hit age thirty with no appreciable prospects, the Cooper women staged an intervention. During Christmas, both my mother and my aunt Colleen pulled me to the side—separately—to say, "You're so hard on men." Apparently, they'd seen one too many a feminist rant on Facebook. Face hot with indignation, I looked at them both pointedly, and said, "This is the woman you raised me to be." "I know," they both told me, in conversations that echoed each other so much I wondered if they had planned it. Despite their fierce investments in being independent, none of these women who raised me had ever struggled with getting or keeping a man. Their critiques made it seem as if I had learned all the wrong things from them. There was an art to "letting a man be a man" and not making him feel intimidated, my mother told me, as she recounted strategies for how to date a man who made less money while not offending his ego. Who has time? Or, better yet, interest? At what point is it fair to ask men to act like grown human beings?

But there is no one more insistent than a mother with a grandbaby agenda. Despite the fact that I have arranged my whole life so that I don't "end up" a single mother like my mother was for most of my life, her current refrain has become, "You could have a baby. You don't have to get married." What is this blasphemy that my good Christian, pastor's wife of a mother is speaking? With every rant she reads on my Facebook page about how brothers need to decolonize their minds, divest from the patriarchy, and cease and desist with the bullshit, my mother can feel her future grandmother status slipping from her grasp, all of it going the way of the few viable eggs that my post-thirty-five body has left. My aunt, on the other hand, the one who has remained single by choice for her entire life, wants me to be lucky in love and to have a partner to go on adventures with. Her partner looks slightly like radio host Tom Joyner and drives a Mercedes convertible. These two perpetual teenagers use this fact to aid and abet their entrance to all the grown-and-sexy post-fifty parties that they go to around town.

If I could loosen up and stop being so mean and ornery, which is Southern-speak for one who takes herself way too seriously, then maybe men could warm up to my charms. All the Cooper ladies mean well, but, on feminist principle, I have to reject any advice that blames sisters for the lack of partnering options. So if it ain't our fault, then whose fault is this shitty state of affairs?

Real talk? I blame Bill Clinton.

I mentioned earlier that some of the baggage Black women carry has to do with the devastating moment when we realize how much our choices around love and marriage are limited by a fucked-up set of social circumstances. I blame Bill Clinton for those social circumstances, and let me tell you why. It is his two terms in office that are most singularly responsible for the structural devastation of Black intimacy and the piss-poor state of Black love, generally, among all of us born after 1980. The presidential election of 2016 became a referendum on Hillary Clinton's support of the Violent Crime Control and Law Enforcement Act of 1994, which her husband signed into law during his first term as president. At the time, Hillary championed her husband's tough-on-crime legislation, parroting an upsurge in rhetoric about the rise of a class of teenage "superpredators." Criminologist John DiIulio, who, at that time, taught at Princeton, began arguing that given skyrocketing rates of violent crimes committed by teens between the mid-1980s and the mid-1990s, the country had a problem on its hands. The number of young Blacks and Latinos would continue to grow, and with them a crime problem the likes of which the country had never seen. Lawmakers concluded that the solution was to lock them up.

When Bill Clinton signed the 1994 crime bill into law, effecting policy at the federal level, it created a ferment of tough-on-crime policies in forty-five states. The crime bill also funded massive increases in police officers across the country. Most striking were laws that allowed juveniles to be tried as adults for violent crimes, and laws that allowed juvenile offenders to receive automatic life sentences for certain crimes.

Moreover, this rhetoric about violent Black male teenagers shaped the social context of my Black male counterparts during our adolescent years. Black boys were being expelled at higher rates than their white male counterparts. Today, Black school-age boys are expelled three times as often as white school-age boys. And black boys in the late nineties were part of the first major wave of the school-to-prison pipeline in which schools pursued zero-tolerance policies for fighting. This meant that Black youth were frequently suspended or expelled and sometimes arrested either for fighting or for truancy. Black male teenagers, boys who were not yet men, became bona fide enemies of the state, the primary targets in law enforcement's war on drugs and crime. The war on Black boys and men was not new. But it reached a fever pitch just as my generation was coming of age.

In the many years since, none of DiIulio's predictions have come true. He and other white male criminologists

stoked the most base fears of white America, and his errone-
ous conclusions devastated the social, economic, and intimate prospects of a whole generation of Black folks—*my*
generation of Black folks. These crime policies took greatest
effect just as people born in the late 1970s and early 1980s
began reaching adolescence and young adulthood. Late Gen
Xers, cusp Millennials or "Xennials" (like myself), and Millennials proper began to use the language of Black men as
an "endangered species" to name the epidemic levels of casualty and out-migration of Black men into prisons that we
witnessed. We believed the myth that there were more Black
men in jail than in college. There never were, but the numbers
were always far too close for comfort. And, of course, there
were more Black women than Black men in college. Howard's ratio in the early 2000s was 3:2, and that was pretty
good among college populations.

These days, DiIulio is notably repentant, having admitted to being wrong. Now he spends a great deal of time
trying to help the very communities that were hurt by the
whack social science that he used to swear by. Twenty years
later, it amounts, for him, to a heavy, if sincere, shoulder
shrug. For those of us young Black people who weathered
the storm, the consequences have been far more severe, far
more sinister. I have spent many a Christmas holiday traveling to even smaller rural areas of Louisiana than the one I
grew up in to visit the many men in my family who have
been victimized by the politics of mass incarceration. I have
watched them attempt to father children, to maintain partnerships, and to hold on to hope from behind bars. I have
seen the endless cotton fields that they spend their days

gazing out upon, in the Podunk backwoods of Louisiana, much like the view that many of our ancestors must have gazed upon 150 or more years ago. And, for those of us making life go on while critical parts of our family units were locked away, I have watched children spiral and struggle, and partners keep vigil, and mothers labor on makeshift altars in prayer, waiting on men they love to come home.

I have also been forced to play a numbers game in the name of love that has increasingly diminished returns for every year that you don't win. And by winning, I mean finding someone to spend your life with. I wish I were mature enough, *feminist* enough, not to think of marriage or the securing of lifelong partnership as a win, or of the absence of these things as a loss, but I do. Despite myself. Sometimes I run the numbers in my head, but this, too, is a double-edged sword. When I see the abysmal state of Black love by the numbers, it's hard to blame myself, but it's hard to have any sense of hope either.

Only 49 percent of Black women with college degrees marry men with some post-secondary education. Fifty-eight percent of married Black women college graduates marry men with an overall lower level of education than they have. Moreover, more than 60 percent of Black women college graduates between the ages of twenty-five and thirty-five, peak childbearing years, have never been married. Compare that number with a mere 38 percent of white women for whom this is true.

According to the Pew Research Center, 36 percent of all Black folks above the age of twenty-five had never been married in the year 2012. In 1960, that number was 9 percent.

For white people, those numbers were 16 percent and 8 percent, respectively. So while the numbers doubled for our white counterparts, they quadrupled for African Americans. The rates of Black men and Black women who have never been married are roughly equal at 36 percent and 35 percent, respectively. But it is Black women who have experienced a far sharper decline in marriageability over the last fifty years. In 1960, 12 percent of Black men over age twenty-five had never been married. And 8 percent of Black women over age twenty-five had never been married. Today the number has tripled for Black men, but more than quadrupled for Black women. Black women who have never married outnumber Black men who have never married at a rate of 100 to 92.

Most women across races list stable employment as a primary factor in whom they choose as a mate. It's not even about a brother needing to be rich. But can he at least have a job and the ability to pay his own bills? When the Pew Research Center accounted for employment status using census data, they found that there are "51 employed Black men for every 100 young Black women." Decades earlier, the numbers were far more equal: There were nearly 90 employed Black men for every 100 young Black women. Here's the rub: "Among never-married white, Hispanic, and Asian American young adults, the ratio of employed men to women is roughly equal—100 men for every 100 women." To add insult to this clear injury, Black folks attach far more importance to marriage than white folks do, and yet we get married far less. Fifty-eight percent of Black folks believe that couples should marry if they plan to spend their lives together. Only 44 percent of white people believe the same thing.

And we haven't even begun to talk about what singleness means for Black women economically. In 2010, the Insight Center for Community Economic Development found that single Black women in the prime working ages of thirty-six to forty-nine have a median net wealth of $5. *Five whole dollars.* Single white women in this same cohort had a net wealth of $42,600. But for every sister who has wished at rent time for a partner with whom to split costs, those numbers get met with our most ardent "Tell us something we don't know."

Given the WTF nature of these statistics, it is absolutely high time that we stop blaming Black women for what is clearly a structural problem. This shit simply is not our fault. Social structures have intimate consequences, and rates of incarceration, employment, and education shape partnering options. Understanding the piss-poor state of Black relationships cannot be reduced to a conversation about individual moral failings. It's not that white folks are less screwed up than we are. It's that they have far more chances to get it right. White people have more access to marriage and partnership because they have more access to absolutely everything else: jobs, housing, safety, and wealth. In my small town, white girls started getting married right out of college. By the time I came home for the ten-year reunion, more of my white classmates were married than not. For my Black women classmates, the situation was exactly the opposite. In the ensuing years, many of these same white girls have gotten divorced. Most of them are seriously dating or have remarried. Most of the Black girls still haven't married husband number one. Having fewer chances to succeed means that you have far fewer chances to fail. It also means that the stakes are ridiculously high every single time a potentially good brother walks through the door.

Those stakes show up when you put up with a man who doesn't treat you right for longer than you should because fear of being alone feels like too much to bear. For Black women, those stakes show up when we date brothers far outside our economic league because we fear being called "bougie," "uppity," and "elitist" if we don't want to give a broke brother a chance. During my first year as a professor, I was out having dinner alone at the local Panera Bread. I frequently take myself out to dinner because, as a single person who doesn't have a typical office job, it often happens that I can go days without seeing anyone of consequence. On this particular night, I was out in my small Southern college town having dinner alone to beat back the loneliness awaiting me at my house. One of the servers came over to sweep the area near me and dropped a note at my booth, calling me cute and asking me for my number on the back of a receipt. Though I had not imagined a brother working for close to minimum wage at Panera to be my best partnering option, my politics demanded that I put aside elitism. He was cute. I said yes.

He took me on a nice date a few days later and seemed interesting and passionate. Because he drove a jalopy, I picked him up and dropped him off at his father's house, where he lived. A few days after that, he asked to come over to my house for a movie night in. When he got there, he said, looking around, pointedly assessing my apartment, "You got a real nice place here." I could see his plans for premature cohabitation starting to take shape. After movies and mediocre sex, the first sex I had had in nearly five years, I never talked to him again. I'm feminist enough to date a brother who makes less money than me. I'm not feminist enough to be any man's plan for a come-up. When I told my mother about him later, she said, "Well, at least he will work." Apparently, this had become the standard—a mere *willingness* to work. And Black men have clear and vocal resentment toward Black women who want brothers with a little money. Kanye made famous these lines: "I ain't saying she a golddigger, but she ain't messin' with no broke niggas."

From the age of twenty to twenty-nine, I was celibate with the exception of a couple of singular and very brief encounters. That is nearly a decade without being touched, desired, complimented, or engaged at any significant intimate level. Dude from Panera got lucky because, at some level, I was not sure when I would again have the opportunity. Among my friends, my years of celibacy aren't anywhere near record-setting. At some point, after you've gone years without a man so much as smiling your way or admiring your looks, you begin to feel invisible. You begin to doubt your own gaze. Recognition is a human need, and there is something fundamentally violent about a world that denies Black women recognition on a regular basis. Even though you look in the mirror and see someone attractive staring back at you, the fact that no one else ever seems to notice fucks with your head. The self-help books that you read before bed tell you that needing external validation is a weakness. You meditate on this while you sleep, but wake craving touch despite your-self. This thirst for compliments is probably why no one is giving them to you. They can see how desperate you are. Desperation is unattractive. You spiral. But what you never do is win. Statistics and analyses about how the patriarchy is beating down your door ain't got nothing on the fervent, insistent desire to get chose.

Black women are eternal optimists. The numbers about absolutely everything except getting diabetes and high blood pressure are never in our favor. We are, therefore, usually un-bowed in the face of a dismal social prognosis. If you're an overachieving Black girl who is used to winning more than losing, on a good day, you imagine that you can bend the odds to your will. On a bad day, you can know the numbers aren't in your favor and still obsess (over wine and Oreos) about why you aren't part of the 51 percent who have a fighting chance. Undaunted by the numbers, the fixing commences. We read the relationship books, go to therapy, dating work-shops, and the annual church singles conference trying to fix ourselves and each other to prepare for ever-elusive oppor-tunities at love. I can ashamedly admit that I was one of the millions of Black women who made comedian Steve Harvey a best-selling author when I ran out and purchased his book *Act Like a Lady, Think Like a Man*. And up until about the year 2012 or so, I saw every single Tyler Perry movie.

Don't make me hand over my feminist card, please. A sister was desperate. It wasn't that I had abandoned my analy-sis of patriarchy. By day, I stepped into classrooms all over campus challenging women and men alike to get on board with feminism. But every night I came home to a pile of lesson planning and an empty apartment. It had become exceedingly clear that my feminist analysis wasn't gonna keep me warm at night or get me laid at all. I needed a regular old straight man, not one with a fancy analysis, to clue me in to how dudes think and what makes them tick. I didn't grow up in the house with men, and I always felt at a disadvantage compared to my few friends who did grow up with father figures in their homes. I saw Tyler Perry's movies and Harvey's book as an opportunity to delve into the emotional lives of Black men. Call it research. I needed to know: *What did brothers want?* When Harvey said every man had a need to profess his love, provide for his mate, and protect her, I recognized this as patriarchal bullshit. For certain. Single for the entirety of my adult life, I had long been confronting things that went bump in the night and providing for myself. And I was proud of my self-sufficiency. My mama taught me to be. But a man professing his love—I needed to know what made them do that. This was valuable insight I needed if I was gonna play the game because, as things stood, I was playing the game quite badly.

For instance, one thing that Harvey proclaimed that I think is true: If a brother hasn't got his career together and has no clear path toward achieving his professional goals, it's hard for that brother to focus on a relationship. It doesn't matter what feminism has to teach us about the structural realities of unemployment and underemployment for Black men. We live in a society that says *real men provide*. And if you are a man who doesn't feel good about his own prospects, then it's hard to think about building with and providing for a partner. Even among those of us feminist chicks who have a more expansive view of these matters, we still want brothers who can share the weight and spend a little money on us sometime.

Recently, I had a lovely first date with a guy named Mike, whom I had met on a dating site. When the check came, I pulled out my wallet to split the bill. One, I'm a feminist and I had kind of pressed Mike to move things offline and into the real world. But if he had actually made me pay, that probably would have been the end of things. Luckily, that night, patriarchy worked in my favor. Mike balked, pushed my hand away, and lightly scolded me, saying, "I don't know what kinda niggas you been dating, but the man *always* pays." At that exact moment, I decided that Mike could get it.

Fast-forward eighteen months later: Mike, a lovely, sweet, thoughtful man comes by for our weekly evening of my home-cooked meals and conversation and cuddle time. We can't see each other too much more than this because he works every available hour and most weekends in order to make a salary that will allow him to financially support himself and his two children. Single, childless, and elated to have the consistent company of a decent man for the first time in my adult life, I remind him that he needs to take me out on a date. It's been months since I last dragged him to a showing of a new romcom. "I know," he says. And I drop it. I'm still trying to find the balance between advocating for myself and not being a nag. At thirty-five, most men have children. If they are decent human beings, they take care of those children, and this means that children and their economic and relational needs are *always* the priority. Like me, Mike grew up without his dad. And, like so many Black men who grew up with the structural shame of the *Moynihan Report* and its denigration of absentee Black fathers, Mike is trying to be superdad. For my part, I feel a mix of admiration and jealousy. This is the first time I am witnessing up close a *man* making the sacrifices to be a present father. I only knew what it looked like watching my mother do it.

I bring up this super-dad thing to Mike as we are leaving a showing of *Southside With You*, a movie that I loved because of the romance and that he loved because he's a Barack stan. We are discussing the scene where Michelle implores Barack to forgive his father for abandoning him. I know Mike has all the sensitive spots about his father having left him as a child. But since movies are (I am hoping) a great way to broach relationship topics that are hard to discuss, I dive in. "It's interesting that brothers our age who didn't have fathers have tried to overcompensate for it with their own kids by becoming super dads," I tell him. "It's interesting because the lesson you learned from your fathers leaving is that you should be better, more dedicated fathers. But none of you thinks anything about learning to be better partners." He looks at me questioningly: "What do you mean?" "Well, the reason your fathers left is often because they didn't know or care to learn how to be good partners to your mothers. I just find it interesting that for a whole generation of you, y'all don't ever think critically about what you should do differently about the partnership piece. So many brothers still resent the mothers of their children, but they insist on being fathers regardless." He says, "Hmmm. I'll have to think about it." And I let the conversation drop, because giving a patriarchy 101 lecture on date night would be tantamount to cock-blocking myself. And this good feminist still needs dick. To put it how Maya Angelou once defined feminism, "It'd be stupid not to be on my own side."

But it occurs to me, as I feign flexibility in the face of canceled dates because of the kids and a reduction in date nights because of economic pressures, that I have no idea how it feels to be a man's number-one priority. After the love was gone, my daddy left, too. And now that I'm dating someone else's daddy, insisting that my needs come first is selfish. But for the first time in my life, I'm at least on the list of priorities. My happiness and my needs are a consideration. This is what I tell my therapist. That what I want more than anything is to know what it feels like to be a consideration. Mike laps at my big-girl body and grabs my booty like he's been waiting all his life to find it. That counts for something, too.

Black men's cultural anxiety about the place of money in relationships is real and palpable. Another brother I dated once asked me, "What do you want in a relationship?" "Well," I told him with an S on my chest, "I don't need a man to give me money or pay my rent or buy me things. I can do that myself." "What *do* you want, then?" he asked rather testily. "I want a *partner,* someone who shows up for me, offers emotional support, and someone to share my life with." "Oh," he said, with no hint of irony, "you want me to be gay!" *This is why we can't have nice things.*

Black men's refusal to own their feelings about how capitalism, patriarchy, and white supremacy leave them shit out of luck on the regular does more harm than good. Scapegoating gay brothers because the heteropatriarchy ain't trying to help straight brothers come up is not the move. And when projecting vulnerability onto gay men doesn't work, too many brothers heap their fear, anxiety, and resentment on Black women. Kanye made millions blaming Black women for desiring men to have some level of economic stability. This anxiety about unstable economic prospects is not new. Black women have been talking about the ways Black men show their asses about this since the 1940s. In 1947, Pauli Murray, a famous civil rights attorney, wrote an article in *Negro Digest* titled "Why Negro Girls Stay Single." She lamented that education was "a social handicap if [the educated woman] wanted marriage." But men didn't date educated women, Murray asserted, "because it would be too great a threat to their security." Patriarchy had made Black men feel like they should be "the lords of creation, the bread-winners and warriors of our time and all time." But given economic realities that limited educational and economic opportunities, the men of Murray's day were mostly stunting while trying to cover up the fact that they were "as frightened and insecure as modern women are."

Fear can distort your view of the facts. Despite the fact that Black women outpace Black men educationally, Black men still have far more net wealth than Black women do. The way patriarchy is set up, men always have more wealth and social status. And this means that marriage has long been the path to economic stability for women of all races. Yet it is Black women who get branded as welfare queens by the government and as gold-digging baby mamas by Black men. At some point, brothers gotta own their shit here. They have to own their fear. They have to own that they have always gauged their nearness to patriarchal dominance by measuring both how far beneath white men they fall *and* how far above Black women they rise. Sisters climbing the social ladder is scary for so many brothers, but it doesn't have to be.

About ten years ago, independent, self-supporting women were in vogue in Black popular culture. Everyone from rapper Webbie to R&B singers Ne-Yo and Jamie Foxx released odes to the independent woman, whom they loved and celebrated because she didn't need a man and had her own money. These brothers seemed to be rejecting Kanye West's anxiety by celebrating the fact that a woman "who got her own" didn't need so much from them. It was a useful intervention, albeit brief. Most brothers I encountered were deeply suspicious of independent women. One brother I dated sat on my couch one night denigrating "all you independent, don't-need-a-man types." When I pointed out the contradiction of hating women who were independent *and* hating women who were "gold diggers" (and therefore by definition, *too* dependent), all I got was a Kanye shrug.

When I was a kid and an angsty teen nerd experiencing my first crushes and my first loves, I believed that Black men loved Black women. If the love songs my mama played on the stereo on Saturday evenings were any indicator, they saw us as gorgeous, magical, and worthy of their best ploys to win our affections. Whether I was listening to my mama's old Luther Vandross tapes or playing Boyz II Men songs on repeat, I understood what it meant for men to profess their love for women in their music. They sang about sex, too, but they also sang about heartbreak, betrayal, unrequited love, and the joy of falling in love. In high school, I lived for the moments when my crushes asked me to slow dance at parties.

By the time I reached my late twenties, slow dancing had gone the way of the rotary phone and love songs had turned into male bitch fests. There is a decided difference between Carl Thomas singing "I wish I never met her at all" and Chris Brown singing "These hoes ain't loyal." Sometimes I wish I could ask Black men "What did we *do* to make you hate us so much?"

I know I sound old, begging for love songs and slow dances. Perhaps I'm asking too much to demand emotional vulnerability and *maturity* from Black men, and at least a smidgen of integrity from those brothers who have access to cultural and religious pulpits. But can we tell the truth about it? Is there a way to say, without sounding like somebody's grandma, that three decades of turning the disrespect of Black women into a global art form via Hip Hop might have some intimate and emotional costs for Black folks? Is there a way to do that without letting white supremacy off the hook for creating the very social conditions that caused these problems in the first place? Where did all this resentment come from? What did Black women ever do to warrant this level of hatred? Where the fuck is the love?

It's seriously so much easier to just blame Bill Clinton.

Late one night, I trekked to Harlem for a series of Emotional Justice conversations that my good friend Esther Armah hosted in an attempt to get Black women and men to be vulnerable with each other in pursuit of mutual healing. I listened to a bunch of ostensibly in-touch, together-brothers dialogue about their feelings, hurts, and traumas and the ways that the failure to think this through in relationships had caused them to do harm to various women. Like many sisters, I sat in the audience all in *my* feelings, grateful for once that maybe there were a few brothers out there willing to share the weight and do some of the emotional labor of building strong Black relationships. Still, the audience that night was 90 percent Black women. There is no justice in that. There can be no justice when brothers fail to show up to have the tough conversations.

There are a few critical shifts that I think we can make that will move us closer together. First, we need to pursue *intimate solidarity* with one another. Solidarity and allyship matter as much in the bedroom as they matter in the revolution. Hip Hop generation brothers love to talk about how their ideal mates are "ride-or-die chicks" who are down for anything. If there is at all a healthy or just version of ride-or-die Black relationships, it is rooted in the concept of being allies and coconspirators. It is rooted in a notion of partnership and solidarity. The way we love each other, or fail to, is a life-and-death situation. Black families and Black communities can't thrive without love in abundance. We need intimate solidarity with one another. Method Man said it this way in the original ride-or-die anthem: "You're all that I need, I'll be there for you. If you keep it real with me, I'll keep it real witchu." This is what intimate solidarity and just Black Love look like—acknowledging that we need each other, committing to showing up for each other, and committing to radical honesty and realness with each other.

Second, Black men have to stop heaping all of their anger and resentment over the way that patriarchy has failed them on the backs of Black women. Far too many brothers conceptualize freedom as the sharing of power with white men. And every time a bid for power fails, it is sisters who get shit upon and who are asked to pick up the broken pieces. This has to change. More to the point, if you feel like your manhood is rooted in failure, how can you possibly love yourself? So much of the discourse of the failure of Black intimacy is about the ways that Black women just need to love themselves. But when we look more closely, very often it is brothers who are oozing wounds of self-hatred and low self-esteem. Any man who treats women as ornamental clearly believes that outward decoration will hide inner deficiency. They have therapists for that.

Third, straight Black men have to stop letting homophobia and misogyny impede healthy possibilities for love. Seeing the desire for partnership as *gay* is teenage-boy logic and it should have no place in the emotional lives of grown men. Homophobia and misogyny will be the death of Black love. Being vulnerable doesn't make one gay *or* straight, and continuing to invest in a view of romantic relationships that is set up for Black folks to lose isn't especially smart. When Black love succeeds in a system that hates us all, there is something profoundly queer about that. Queer Black folks have survived precisely because they have refused to let traditional ideas about what love and relationships should look like dictate what is possible for them.

Partnership, and all of the practices that are necessary to achieve it, disrupt the social hierarchies that currently structure Black intimacy. Partnership demands that we meet each other on equal footing. Partnership stops placing the entire onus on Black men to profess, protect, and provide. That's too much weight to carry. We all need someone to speak up for us, to look out for us, and to share resources to help us make it. We bring all our strengths and our weaknesses to the table. We agree that no matter what we ride for each other. We decide that we are coconspirators in a project of Black love. We agree to do the work we need to do to be together. We center a justice practice as a love language. We commit to being intimately and relationally just with one another.

If my grandmother could see this lay of the land, I think she would say, "You young folks study yourselves way too much!" In other words, we overthink everything and take it all so deadly seriously. We have to figure out how to commit to the fierce pursuit of joy with one another. There was a boy whom I thought I loved, a Southern country boy intellectual, who seemed like the prototype of the kind of man I thought I should marry. Randy was the kind of dude who could quote Black feminist theorists like bell hooks and Patricia Hill Collins off the dome. We were intellectual kindred spirits. He had a reputation for being a ladies' man, though, and once when we were honest enough to joke about it, he said to me, "I'm a feminist. I *love* women." During one conversation, in the spring of 2008, when it looked like Barack Obama would have a real chance of clinching the Democratic nomination, I had lunch with Randy. He said, "I don't understand why Michelle Obama hasn't quit her job yet." Looking curiously at him, I asked, "Well, why would she? He isn't the nominee yet." And in the parlance of a church boy, he said, "Yes, but surely it's time for her to get fully on board with his vision." In that moment I knew that, while Randy was a feminist intellectually, his first impulse emotionally was to expect a high-powered career woman like Michelle Obama to quit *her* job, to support her husband going after *his* dreams. That wasn't feminist. Lots of men have feminist rhetoric down, but many of them haven't done the emotional work of showing up for a woman with dreams and visions of her own. I learned in that moment that marrying a feminist dude wasn't the goal. Instead, I learned to look for men who genuinely *like* and value women as people.

Years later, though, I saw the girl Randy did marry. A lovely woman with a career of her own, who prioritized supporting his career. None of this surprised me. But the thing I also discovered was that she made him laugh uproariously on the regular. I realized that even though my assessments about the legitimacy of his feminist politics were right, and our intellectual kinship mattered, in the end he chose a partner with whom he could find unadulterated joy. And in this, too, is a lesson. Given the hard realities that Black folks face in finding their way to one another, Black love is nothing if it is not simultaneously a conduit to Black joy. The lessons seem to be: Find someone who makes you laugh. Find someone who doesn't allow you to take yourself too seriously. Find someone who brings you joy. And please, please bring back slow dancing.

FAVOR AIN'T FAIR

Survivor's guilt shows up in a really odd way among Black radical intellectuals. The ongoing narrative in Black social justice and academic spaces is that working-class Black neighborhoods—the hood, the ghetto, the projects—are revolutionary. One activist told me during a training for organizers that it was the job of Black professionals, those of us who had "made it," to return to the live in the hood.

I lived for four of my first five years in the projects. I remember it. And while the projects in the small-town South are not at all comparable to the horror stories I hear coming out of urban ghettos, I have no intention of returning. And I don't have any guilt about it. The activist who insisted that I should want to return is himself first-generation middle class. His parents grew up in the hood, and he suffered from a serious case of FOMO. His solution was that we should all, therefore, return.

I, on the other hand, witnessed exactly what the daily

grind looked like for my mother, who had the nerve to have middle-class aspirations as she slowly, methodically worked her way from a place in the projects to a modest apartment to a house. When I was about four, my mom, dad, and I went to the A&P grocery store. My mom, still in her work clothes, looked bone tired. As the groceries sailed down the conveyor belt, my dad stood at the other end. When time came to pay, only my mother reached for her wallet. I looked at Daddy, expecting, thinking, waiting on him to contribute. He looked at me sheepishly, almost shrugging, as my mother paid for the groceries alone. Why hadn't my daddy helped my mommy?

In the months to come, Daddy bounced, strutting out the door one sunny morning, with a white towel slung over the shoulder of his bare torso, after my mother summoned the courage to tell him "It's over." He left without incident, refusing even to catch my eye as I sat on the sofa, witnessing his exit.

I asked my mother what motivated her to want to get out of the projects, even though all of her friends still lived there. She said simply, "I saw people going to sleep all around me. I wanted better for you." Concentrated poverty meant that seeing ambulances and hearing police sirens were a regular occurrence. One evening, one of mama's friends showed up holding a bloody T-shirt in a bag. Her brother had been stabbed and, though he would be fine, she had gone to the hospital to collect his belongings. I knew her brother, and I was horrified to see the bloody contents of that bag dangling from her hands while she stood in our living room.

There is often little peace and quiet and even less space to think when violence can show up in your living room at

any given time. I told the young activist who began to bel-
ligerently insist on his revolutionary hood housing program
that asking Black women to move back into violent, under-
resourced spaces didn't seem particularly revolutionary to
me. His revolution was rooted in a male-centered conception of men politicking in the ghetto. But Black women's
revolutions are always about safety, food, and education for
women, children, and the elderly. No matter where the sisters
are, we are always making meals, raising children, and keeping things together. When we do make it out, we make it out
in the simple hopes that it will be a little easier to keep things
together now. Guilting Black folks, particularly Black women,
for pursuing safety, care, and possibility for their children
is not a freedom project.

When my mother announced casually while putting
away laundry in our apartment, "We're getting a house," I
jumped on her back, hugging her, shrieking for joy. This was
a big deal, even though she was playing it cool.

When we pulled up to the house, I vaguely remembered
that I had seen Chip Brown, the little brother of Tami Brown
(the girl who had called me "nigger"), peering out from the
screen door of this very house, the year before when my school
bus passed through the neighborhood. After they had moved
out, my mother's realtor had come and cried, she'd told my
mother, over the mess they'd made of the place. On the Sat-
urdays leading up to our move, I helped wash the walls at
our new house while Mama climbed on the kitchen counters,
unscrewed all the old cabinets, stripped the old varnish from
them, and replaced it with a shiny new coat. During breaks,
I rolled my eight-year-old body on the new blue carpet,

thinking it felt so nice compared to the dingy brown carpet in the apartment we were leaving.

Those were the triumphs. But the stress showed up, too, in the form of my mother's perpetually upset stomach, her painful and chronic ingrown toenails that there was no money to fix, and the kind of strictness that occurs when you don't have time for your child to do anything but toe the line. My mother believed in old-school parenting, which meant she didn't believe it was her job to entertain me. "That is why you have a room full of books and toys," she would pointedly remind me every time I complained too much about being bored. Getting Mama to play board games with me, or to let me play in her hair and call her by her first name were treats reserved for special days.

I became an exceptional student, because it was the only job I had. My mother went to work to make a life for us, and I went to school and made A's. A's made my mother proud, and I was a classic overachieving only child, deeply adult-identified and invested in keeping my mother happy. Getting A's was not rewarded. That was the expectation. When it became clear to my community—family members, teachers, church congregation—that I was an exceptionally smart child, the refrain of my interactions with these adults became "Get your lesson, girl! Keep your head in them books! If you put God first, you can go anywhere and be anything." I loved all the positive attention, and brought home all the A's I could to keep it going.

Being singled out as exceptional by the adults at home and school created its own set of problems among my peers. I became a target of other Black children in the community, who accused me of "talking too proper" and "acting white." From their vantage point, I was trying to be special and different, in ways that they either could not be or did not want to be. One Saturday, two girls from down the street came to visit. We weren't friends entirely, but we were cool. It was almost as if Dominique and Trecie had been given a dare to come knock on my door and see what would happen. I let them in and took them to my very girly room, with the pink-and-blue doll wallpaper and peach bedspread, the Barbie dolls and Baby-Sitters Club books, the notebooks and papers where I played school with said dolls, strewn about. Out of sheer Southern politeness, we engaged in banal chatter, with it all feeling entirely odd to me. These girls were not my friends. Why were they at my house? Finally, after this performance had gone on for a few minutes, Dominique looked at me with pity and said, "You really do want to be white, don't you?"

"Well, no," I stumbled, taken aback, offering a none-too-impressive response. Dominique humored me, nodding as I talked. She still thought I was weird, though. They had caught me at home on a weekend in a place where I wasn't used to being attacked. At school, where my guard was always up, when I was taunted, I usually shouted back "Does being smart make you white?" Witty retorts were not my specialty. After a few more minutes of awkwardness, Dominique and Trecie left. Meanwhile, an opportunity to connect with some Black girls for friends had slipped away yet again. I sat in my room, wondering what was wrong with the kind of Black girl I chose to be, and also thinking they were supremely ignorant for believing that a love of books and standard English meant I wanted to be white.

Year upon year of being called white only strengthened my resolve for an exit strategy. My mother hated that I was so bothered. She came home and talked to me about an article she had read that said we all have different ways of talking, depending on the audience. I eagerly sucked up this information, hoping that I didn't secretly really want to be white. But somehow, other Black girls didn't recognize the Tevin Campbell and Boyz II Men–loving Black girl in me. On particularly bad days, my mama would give me the Black mama pep talk. "Those kids ain't 'bout nothing. You stay focused. And if you keep on living, one of these days, you'll see how they turn out, versus how you turn out."

She was right, of course. Our paths were largely set by the time we were nine. My teacher, Mrs. Gaulden, one of only a very few Black teachers that I had, insisted that I be tested for the Gifted and Talented program. When the results came in and she was told that I had failed, she insisted they rescore my test. They had, in fact, made an error. I was indeed gifted and talented and, therefore, worthy of small, special classes and extracurricular experiences. Many of my classmates, especially those without benefit of Mrs. Gaulden, received no such special care, cultivation, or opportunities.

Many of those children continued to labor under the assumption that white people, and we Blacks who supposedly wanted to be white, had a monopoly on smartness. Nothing about our deeply segregated school system ever challenged their ideas. And, of course, my weak retorts to the daily taunts did not ever rise to the level of a piercing systemic critique. I came to believe that I was special, unique, and exceptional. Of course, I wanted to be among smart Black overachieving kids. This is why I set out for Howard at the first opportunity. But making it out of Ruston, Louisiana, meant that I had to believe the lie of my own exceptionalism—that my classmates had fewer opportunities because they didn't try hard enough and because they were trying to be too cool for school.

At one point in high school, my godsister April joined in on taunting me. We had grown up together, my mother the best of friends with her mother and her aunts. April grew up in the "old projects" while I lived a few blocks away in the "new projects." The only thing that really distinguished them was that the new projects had lighter bricks and metal screen doors, while the old projects had wooden ones. By high school, April had her crew, and I had mine. No one knew we had grown up as damn near kin, that we used to sleep in the same bed together while the adults went down to a club called The Limb to dance the night away. One aunt always stayed behind and threatened us late into the night, telling us, "Take your asses to bed before I come in there and whup somebody!"

On this day, I watched as April giggled at me as other girls, her friends, tossed barbs my way, berating everything from the way I talked to my long, straight hair. "She *need* a perm," one of them taunted as April giggled. During my daily debriefing with my mother, I mentioned that some girls at school said I needed a perm. "They're just jealous," my mother said. Back then, I had an enviable head of long, thick, Black-girl hair that was great for styling. But I was mostly oblivious to it, since I much preferred to have my head in a book than in a stylist's chair. I mentioned the names of the girls taunting me, thinking nothing of including April. It had been years since we'd spent weekends having sleepovers while our parents were out on the town. My mother called her aunt and told it. And April, I heard, got the dressing-down of her life, as every single auntie let her know that "not only do you not need to be picking on Brittney, but you need to be trying to do what she doing." Apparently, being fussed out was effective. The very next time this scenario went on in the hallway, I looked her in the eye, anticipating the barbs, but she was curiously, noticeably, silent. I was relieved. I hadn't really planned to rat her out, but I appreciated the affirmation that the adults in her life gave me: "You need to be doing what Brittney is doing."

Being excluded and being exceptional are the frequent prerequisites for a bad case of self-righteousness. Because I was a classic *good girl*, I naturally thought myself more devout and more Godly than my classmates, and when that is combined with an evangelical orientation to the world, it's a problem. I approached knowing God the same way I approached getting A's. Follow the rules, and success will come to you. The more I excelled, the more I chalked it up to God's blessing and "favor" on my life. Black church folks love to talk about how "blessed and highly favored they are." It is the kind of explanation that comes to stand in, far too often, for structural inequality. *Favor ain't fair.* Or so the saying goes. So I came to understand my success in that way, too. In my early twenties, a preacher at my local church went so far as to prophesy blessings of God's favor over my life. I had been put here to make a special impact, he pronounced one evening during a Bible study class.

Here's the thing: I'm still a Christian. So I will never dis-
count God's favor and the way it has shown up in my life.
This is a challenge for mainstream feminism, because much
of it is still a deeply secular project. So many Black women I
know, even those who don't go to church very much, still
have deep spiritual and religious lives. Most Black feminists
I know have some version of a God-concept. For those of us
who watched our mamas work themselves damn near to
death to raise up powerful daughters like us, attributing it to
sheer strength of will and hard work is an American fable that
doesn't suit us. Liberal white folks tell themselves these kinds
of stories—that they made it because of their own ingenuity
and will. But most Black girls have enough humility to see
ourselves as walking miracles who, as Audre Lorde famously
said, "were never meant to survive." I want to be clear that
God has a place in how I think about justice and feminism,
but I hate God-explanations for structural problems. I learned
the limits of these kinds of explanations clearly when I returned to reckon with my old classmates at the ten-year high
school reunion.

There was no way I was missing the reunion. This was
my victory lap, and I was just petty enough to take it. I was
a few months shy of completing my doctorate and had ful-
filled the promise of my senior designation in the yearbook:
"most likely to succeed." My friend Reina, one of the two
mean girls from middle school, accompanied me. We had
grown up around the corner from each other, ours a friendship borne of necessity, since we were two of three Black girls
routinely taking honors courses together. It wasn't so much
that we got along back then as we needed each other to

get along. We had weathered the storm of our teenage years, and, with the angst and competition behind us, we had become real friends. We were a team on reunion night. Racial politics back home being what they are, there came a moment at the end of the homecoming football game (think *Friday Night Lights*) when the entire class decided to go out for a drink. Once we reach adulthood in the small town where I went to high school, Black and white folks don't really socialize at the same watering holes together to any great degree. Reina and I stood in the bleachers, watching our classmates split by race. We looked at each other, wondering which group we should choose. The Black kids hadn't been our friends, but the very Republican evangelical whiteness of our classmates wasn't as palatable as it had been a decade before. We figured we might as well throw our lot in with the Blacks.

So, we went to a local restaurant for drinks. I threw back a couple of shots of Tequila and started dancing to a Hip Hop song blaring over the speakers. A new dance was out, and as is the custom of folks who are getting grown, we were trying to figure out who could, in fact, "do tha stanky leg." Lashay looked at me and said, "I want Brittney to do it!" It was a gentle, mocking challenge, one designed to literally have me prove my Blackness once and for all, by standing up and dancing for the group. *This bullshit again. Seriously?* "I'm not that drunk," I told Lashay. Ten years had helped my comeback game moderately.

But since she had, I reasoned, started it, I refused to let it go. As our food came, I said to the table, "It's just so interesting that I'm here. Because the narrative was that I wanted to be white back in the day." Lashay nodded. "That *is* true.

People did say that." Lavonne jumped in, hoping to keep the peace and not fuck up the vibe, saying, "Awww, you know we were just jealous." *Jealous? Jealous?!* Jealous. There was that word again. And I was as incredulous about it then as I had been years before, when my mama offered it as an explanation for the actions of April and her friends.

April didn't make it to the ten-year reunion. She had died suddenly of natural causes, a few days after giving birth to her daughter, during the fall of my freshman year of college. Thankfully, we'd made our peace the summer before I left when I ran into her at Wendy's, where she worked. She was a few months' pregnant and I was heading off to college. Somehow, we both moved along the trajectories that my town seems to set up for Black girls. Either you become an exceptional achiever, or you settle into a life of low-wage work and children. Exceptionalism or struggle should not be the only pathways available to Black people. When my mother talked about watching "where those girls would end up," I know she had not, in fact, been thinking of April. April saw me, smiled, and said, "Hey, Brittney." I smiled back. Childhood beefs were squashed, and we were both moving into our respective paths of womanhood.

Jealousy was the one emotion that I had never ever expected to hear. It had never occurred to me that the Black children in my school knew there was something wrong with a system that singled out a few exceptional children and gave them the keys to the kingdom. I took a moment. Then I replied, "Man, I'm not holding on to it. We were all victims of a fucked-up system. It chose particular kids and gave them everything. And it was set up to make us think that the white kids were so much smarter, while really it was simply that they got more attention, more resources, and more opportunities. I don't blame y'all for that. These people in this town are racist." Lavonne nodded her head. And we went back to drinking.

Out in the car, Reina looked at me and said, "I don't agree at all with how you handled that. You let them off the hook! And they made our childhoods miserable!" I had. And they had. Though Reina and I had grown up in the same neighborhood, with single mamas hustling to make a living for us, we resolved the trauma very differently. For a long time she took their internalized anti-Blackness as evidence that there was little room for her in Black communities. She gravitated toward white friends, multicultural Christianity, and conservative values. I went to Howard, found thousands of the overachieving, nerdy Black kids I'd been looking for, and healed because I began to experience a world in which smart Black folks just made sense. I was able to see my childhood, the bullying, and small-mindedness as a function of retrograde racial politics that became magnified in the context of a small town in the semirural deep South. More than that, I had learned the pitfalls of using a respectability framework to explain the achievement gap in our communities. Before going away to college, I thought other Black children were lazy, unmotivated, and ignorant, and I ultimately concluded that they had gotten what they deserved. But at the reunion, Lavonne offered me new insight. When she framed their childhood disdain toward me as jealousy, what I heard, more precisely, was an awareness of an injustice. Black children know when they are being left behind, devalued, and overlooked.

Black communities have always been aware of the prickly politics of racial exceptionalism. W.E.B. Du Bois famously advocated for Black communities to train what he called the "Talented Tenth," an exceptional core of leaders who would get access to education and resources and bring them back to everyone else. More progressive Black thinkers have long rejected the elitism of Talented Tenth–based leadership models. These models favor Black folks who are polished, articulate, and easily able to acclimate to white environments. There was the pressing danger of Talented Tenth types returning to their home communities and looking down upon everyone else as unsophisticated, unintelligent, and self-destructive. But while Du Bois thought of this as a pragmatic strategy in a world where white people were not invested in being broadly inclusive, many of the Blacks who came to have this kind of access felt entitled to it. Thus, part of the consciousness-raising process on the radical Black left has been to be deeply suspicious of anything that looks like class-based entitlement. Moreover, young radical brothers, like the one who tried to convince me to move back to the hood, located their radicalism in the completion of Du Bois's strategy. It had failed because too many of us refused to go back. All would be well if the educated few would return and lend their talents to the struggling Black masses. But liberation is never so simple as getting it and bringing it back. Any educated sister who sends a considerable chunk of her paycheck home to the folks who haven't yet made it out will tell you that we leave and return to the places that made us, many times over the course of a lifetime.

Still, our guilt over leaving people behind nips at our heels, at every new station that we reach. For instance, whenever there is a convening at an academic conference, invariably some young radical person will get on the mic to ask, "Who isn't in the room? Who are we excluding?" These questions matter, but they can also be deeply annoying because very often they are a performance of middle-class angst. These people know full well who won't be at the conference before they ever sign up to come to it. How do we balance the impulse to think that having degrees equips us to speak *for* people in their absence with the fact that the degrees in most cases actually do mean we have something of value to contribute that we might not otherwise have had? My grandmother, who never finished high school, stayed on me to "get my lesson," because she knew there was something of value in the books I so loved to read. She knew it, and those of us who have read those books know it, too. Why do we patronize people by acting like our access to more education didn't actually teach us anything of value? That's a patronizing lie we have to stop telling, for it serves no one and insults the very folks who made the sacrifices for us to get here.

On one too many occasions I have had social justice–oriented folks chide me for being elitist while they were diligently grinding their way through graduate programs at institutions far more elite than the ones I have attended. Part of what I am saying is that the anxiety about being inclusive is itself a middle-class Black anxiety, a fear we have of getting too big for our britches, so to speak. Some of us handle our guilt by blaming it on God and His mysterious and divine favor and intentions. Others romanticize the very conditions they have spent their whole lives escaping. How do we deal with our guilt when we are the ones who achieved in a system that is intentionally set up for most Black folks to fail?

I don't know that I have the answer to that question. But I do know that we annoy the hell out of each other with assertions of our connections to various hoods, and blocks, and working-class communities. An accusation that one is elitist is like the sounding of the death knell to any activist or scholar committed to the struggle. It's akin to somebody rolling up and dissing your mama. But there is a gender dynamic to it. When I have experienced these kinds of accusations from other Black feminist women, typically, it's mean-girl shit and jealousy masquerading as a radical critique. When Black men do it to Black women, it is a way to deny Black women the authority of being legitimate theorists or decision makers within Black communities. The absurdity of this is that most of us are only 1.5 generations, at most, into the Black middle class. The vast majority of educated Black folks aren't that far removed from the mythic "Cousin Pookie" whom Obama was obsessed with forcing off the sofa and into the voting booth. But President Obama's invocation of "Cousin Pookie," a stereotype signaling disengaged and disaffected young Black men, was an intentional bid for street cred through an appeal to a cultural narrative accessible primarily to Black folks. President Obama wanted us to believe that he knew a Cousin Pookie or two himself. The ability to claim proximity to such folks is just one way that elite and middle-class Blacks index their continued insider status in working-class Black communities. It's highly problematic, mostly because it's performative, and not just on Obama's part. In other words, this kind of fronting doesn't help anybody. The sisters I know remain connected to their working-class roots because the extra money we do make is often used to help somebody back home make the rent or car note, pay for Ma'Dear's light bill or medications, or just give whoever needs it a few extra dollars to tide them over till the next payday. Black women's consistent philosophy is "If we eat, everybody eats." If I'm not struggling, no one in my family struggles either. It is precisely this thinking that leads to Black women my age having a median net wealth of $5.

Favor *isn't* fair. So we should have what womanist theologians call a "hermeneutic of suspicion"—a healthy skepticism—of the institutions and opportunities that would make of us exceptions. Relying on the favor of God to open doors for us is not a plan for systemic change or justice at any broad level. And using the favor of God to justify the machinations of a system that routinely forecloses opportunities for Black women's thriving ain't revolutionary, either. In fact, if this framework of favor goes unchecked it lays the groundwork for an unholy trinity between the church, neoliberalism, and racial respectability politics. Black preachers point to the work of currying favor with God by obeying all the rules the Bible sets out because, to them, God's favor is more powerful than any systemic obstacle. At their best, Christian invocations of favor are used as a resource in the fight against routine injustices that harm Black people and deny them access to opportunity. One problem, though, is that this approach to currying favor with God is individual. Second, it is wholly dependent upon the dictates of respectability politics to work.

God apparently grants favor first and foremost to those who follow the rules—those who tithe 10 percent of their income, those who don't have sex before marriage, those who attend church and Sunday school faithfully, those who don't think sinful thoughts, those who don't struggle with addictions of any sort, those who strive for perfection, and those who are always on their best behavior. It turns out that schools favor those who follow these rules, too. In shorter form, success comes to those who take *personal responsibility* for their lives. But following the rules shouldn't be the guarantor of rights or dignity.

Black children and Black people are told that if they simply follow the rules, they can make it into the middle class, where the hope is that they will experience some level of stability. When this respectability formula links up with Christian dogma about God's favor, one comes to believe that their access to a stable social life, with the ability to pay their bills, have secure and affordable housing, healthy and affordable meals, good public schools, and a bit of discretionary income is a function of God's blessing and favor. Those who rely on God's favor to secure what the system cannot provide unwittingly admit that they know the system is a fraud. They know things are not set up for Black folks to win. But since God wants us to win as long as we do right, then theology becomes a substitute for demanding that the system be more just.

In this way the church, as I mentioned in my discussion of grown-woman theology, has become complicit in the

broader project of neoliberalism, which is marked by a social abdication of responsibility to create systems that help
the vast majority of citizens achieve some notion of the
good life. Instead, neoliberalism turns our attention to individual self-regulation, and notions of personal empowerment,
as the pathway to having anything in life. And yet, again, what
we teach and preach in churches allows "God" language to
do the dirty work of the system, namely, pretending to empower us while ultimately blaming our lack of social options
on some flaw in our character or misstep in our conduct.

I very much had to resist the narrative that I made it
because I acted right. Racist teachers humiliated me and
tried to break my spirit, *even when I acted right.* Acting right,
which far too often means "acting white," didn't protect me
from what Carol Anderson calls the "white rage" of my classmates when they realized that I actually would graduate at
the top of the class, and atop all of them. And plenty of Black
children who acted right still didn't have the levels of opportunity I had.

Part of the work of justice for those of us who made it out
of terribly fucked-up conditions is rejecting the myth of our
own exceptionalism. That is the thing I tried to do at the
table in the conversation with my classmates. I tried to find
common cause with them, despite the traumas they enacted
on me. Black people can do terrible harm to each other when
we aren't clear who the enemy is. But in finding common
cause I also wanted to avoid doing harm to my community,
to not participate in the narrative that stripped children
who were just like me of having real educational opportunity, simply because they didn't, for instance, show an early

facility for reading. I wanted to forgive my childhood tormentors, and at the same time to put some of the fancy educational analysis that I'd had the benefit of receiving to good and just use.

The idea that the pathway to freedom is found in better choices is bullshit. Take, for instance, the latest research on the racial wealth gap. Any time I'm in racial justice organizing spaces at least one brother demands the mic so that he can tell us that "What Black people need to do is support Black businesses. If we would just pool all our resources and stop spending money on Jordans and hair weaves, we could have real wealth to invest in our communities." The research says differently. Black people at every level spend less money than white folks in similar economic circumstances. It turns out that the entire respectability formula for raising Black socioeconomic status is a fail. Going to college, raising children in a two-parent home, working full-time, and spending less do not make it possible for Black people to close the wealth gap that they have with white people. White people have more money because their ancestors made money from owning our ancestors. When white people die, other white people gain wealth. When black folks die, they often leave debt behind.

When my grandmother died a decade ago, the bank let us know that she had a safe-deposit box. We went expecting that there would be an insurance policy, a will, and other information about her assets. Instead we found an unceremonious collection of thirty-year-old receipts from the phone company. Grandmama took pride in paying her bills, and in owing "nary a debt." That was her legacy; that she died owing no one anything. So many Black folks aren't that lucky, and death often means loved ones inherit the debt of those who've passed on. In every generation, the vast majority of Black people must start over trying to build wealth. Sometimes they can only do that after they've resolved the debts others have left for them to handle.

In order for people to make healthier, more sustainable choices that will support their thriving, they have to have better options. But the Hail Mary politics of divine favor (i.e., using favor like a Hail Mary) ain't about having more options, but rather about what happens when you have far too few of them. The hood is marked by a lack of access to reasonable options. It always annoys me to find out that the woke, radical, pro-Black, feminist position is uncritical valorization of the hood. Let me say this: If the people on the block had the answers, the revolution would have long since come. Disproportionate numbers of our people are locked in the structural hopelessness that attends concentrated poverty. Many of them dissent from that hopelessness every day by making a way anyway, by using their own ingenuity and will to create options for themselves where none exist.

Being asked to do more with less is inhumane. Frequently, social scientists point to the resilience of children from difficult backgrounds. One time, in a meeting on my campus, in a discussion about the hardships children of color face, a white woman remarked dismissively, "Oh, but children are resilient!" Celebrating the resilience of poor folks is a perverse way of acknowledging the unreasonable demands placed upon people who already are struggling to make it. In fact, in this moment, when a broad-scale conservative backlash threatens to absolutely gut the social safety net, "resilience" is a dangerous word. The logic of relying on people's resilience goes something like, "Let's see just how much we can take away from you before you break." That shit is evil. We can celebrate and recognize the awesome ways that Black humanity and possibility show up without drinking the Kool-Aid.

My mother is my shero. I'm the biggest beneficiary of her ingenuity and tenacity. But I don't mistake the model my mother carved for me for a liberation plan for all Black people. Nor is it reasonable to blame all the folks who didn't do what she did for their own social condition. You can't judge the effectiveness of a system by the success of its exceptional actors, from the president on down.

So, what do we do when the woke position demands that we cosign ways of thinking that actually don't make any sense? My entire life, my community encouraged me to leave and make something of myself. As soon as I achieved the highest possible credentials, suddenly lots of brothers, some with degrees and many more who didn't finish school, started popping up, mansplaining that "Even though you might be more educated than me, that doesn't mean you have more knowledge than me." Some of the smartest folks I've ever known didn't have college degrees. As I've said, my daddy was the smartest man I never knew. I can throw a rock and hit an educated fool. But this suspicion of education and its benefits is part of a broader culture of American anti-intellectualism that we simply must reject. From age four to age twenty-eight, save one year, I was a student. Ten of those years were spent in pursuit of higher education. This counts for something. The one year that I wasn't a student, I worked at a public school. If I had already learned everything I would need to know in my community of origin, then all of the Black folks in that community would not have encouraged me to reach for the skies.

Thus, when I see other radicals with elite access valorizing their hoods, I recognize it as misapplied survivor's guilt and a deep desire to retain one's street cred and authenticity. Whenever we're together, highly educated folks start doing this dance of talking about how we really need to appreciate what the hood taught us. I've done some of this dance myself, and much of it I believe in. Theorizing all the possibilities of resistance in crunk music and ratchet television is good, important cultural work, rooted in the working-class sensibilities of the South. Appreciating the epistemological frameworks, the ways of knowing and making sense of the world that my grandmother and my mother bequeathed to me is radical work that upends the politics of the academy as the only place where anyone is saying anything of value. But. The ignobility of academe doesn't make the hood noble.

I gained the tools to do better analytic work and ask better questions *in* the university. I became a feminist in a Ph.D. program. Hell, I learned the word *epistemology* in a Ph.D. program. But, more than all of that, I learned to heal from the anti-Black trauma and bullying that was the entirety of my childhood *at college*. The first day I stepped into Professor Lawrence Jackson's honors composition classroom was the first day of my life that I wasn't presumed to be the smartest Black person in my classroom. Suddenly I was in the middle of 360 degrees of Black brilliance and, briefly, I was *shook*. Who was I, if "smart Black girl" fit fully 60 percent of the people on campus? Suddenly I was no longer the only one, a truth I gulped down while I looked around the room at all the other eager students listening to Dr. Jackson's lecture about why the map of the world made Africa look so much smaller than everywhere else when, really, it was larger.

The trap and the burden of being exceptional is that your entire identity is wrapped up in being the only one. The stories of infighting and competitiveness among Blacks that we tell when we get together have everything to do with building an identity based on being the exception. It took exactly one day at a Black college to break me of such thinking. It was both scary and exhilarating, but I came to understand the racial politics of U.S. public schools in my college and grad-school classrooms. Those frameworks gave me what I needed to go back and see that my classmates and I had been victims of a system that pitted us against each other as a justification for its own logic of white dominance and Black exceptionalism. American democracy is not interested in acknowledging that a Barack Obama can be found in every Black community. I have met brilliant Black boys at every step of my journey. Many of them were languishing in poor schools and even worse neighborhoods. Just like there are many, many white men who make viable candidates for the presidency, the same is true for Black communities. The only difference is structural levels of access, not levels of talent or intellect. I would not have known that if I had not left my community.

And, despite what I know now, I still remember the loneliness of being a Black-girl nerd longing for community for most of my childhood. I forgive my bullies, but I don't want to live in any sustained community with them. Over the years, most of the specific incidents of harm have faded. But whenever I run into one of my old tormentors around town, typically I know because my stomach twists and turns into knots, recoiling at slights that have long since passed. That's a truth to sit with, too: The harm is no less harmful simply because we know what caused it. Structural violence is rooted in the need to maintain hierarchies, but far too often its most gut-wrenching acts are enacted horizontally, by our peers, not by those positioned above us. Real radicalism implores us to tell the whole ugly truth, even when it's inconvenient. To own the hurt and the pain. To own our shit, too. To think about it systemically and collectively, but never to diminish the import of the trauma.

Survivor's guilt is about as useful as white guilt, which is to say, not useful at all. My mama worked too hard and my community prayed too much for me to feel guilty about making it. But I have copious amounts of rage at the systems that refused to nurture the talents of the kids who looked like me. And more than that, I have a great sense of responsibility. I'm not planning to go back home to live, because where I'm from is no place for a radical feminist Black girl who likes to challenge preachers in her spare time. But I am responsible in big and small ways for making that place and places like it better, more equitable and more just. I'm thankful for favor, such as it is, but I refuse to mistake favor for freedom. Knowing more than the folks with less education than you, doesn't mean you know everything. In some cases, it doesn't even mean you know the best things or the right things. But education *is* powerful. That is ancestral wisdom that our folks fought for us to have. We don't serve them well by acting like we don't know anything worth knowing. Going off to college and to grad school turned me into a picket-sign carrying, Jesus-loving radical feminist. I stand by the notion that the ideas I learned in those places, and that all the things Black feminism has taught me, can help our folks get free. And for all who would disagree I would say, simply, "Ain't no future in our frontin'."

JOY

The term "feminist killjoys" is well-earned. Sometimes, in the bid for *rightness*, feminists and hyperwoke folks can take the joy out of everything. I actually think it's irresponsible to wreck shop in people's world without giving them the tools to rebuild. It's fine to quote Audre Lorde to people and tell them, "The master's tools will never dismantle the master's house." The harder work is helping people find better tools to work with. We have to smash the patriarchy, for sure. And we have to dismantle white supremacy, and homophobia, and a whole bunch of other terrible shit that makes life difficult for people. Rage is great at helping us to destroy things. That's why people are so afraid of it.

But part of what I've been trying to say is that rage can help us build things, too. The clarity that comes from rage should also tell us what kind of world we want to see, not just what kind of things we want to get rid of. I'm not interested in a feminist project that only works to tear down things. Black women know that justice is rarely found in the rubble. If your rage can do anything for you, I hope it can do for you what it has done for me—help us to build the world we want to see.

And since, as you know by now, I'm a church girl, I want to end this book in the way that I've watched Black preachers end church services my entire life. I want to offer you a benediction. My stepdad, a Baptist preacher and the first pastor I ever had, told us that we should never leave church without the benediction. Those good words spoken at the end imbued us with power to go out and live out the things we had just learned about.

So here goes . . .

May you have joy.

Joy, as I have heard countless Black preachers say, is different from happiness, because happiness is predicated on "happenings," on what's occurring, on whether your life is going right, and whether all is well. Joy arises from an internal clarity about our purpose. My purpose is justice. And the fight for justice brings me joy.

In your president's favorite book of the Bible, Two Corinthians, these words appear: "We are hard-pressed on every side, but not crushed; perplexed, but not in despair; persecuted, but not abandoned; struck down, but not destroyed." In shorter form, the Black Church would say, "Joy—the world didn't give it to me, and the world can't take it away." Maintaining the capacity for joy is critical to the struggle for justice. Things are still as fucked up at the end of this book as they were at the beginning. But we can't let the messed-up state of the world steal our joy.

It is critical in reinvigorating our capacity for new visions. When we lack joy, we have a diminished capacity for self-love and self-valuing and for empathy. If political struggle is exercise for the soul, joy is the endorphin rush such struggles bring.

May you have gut-busting belly laughter, every day.

Laughing with my girls brings me joy. Traveling around the world, migrating down South to my mama's sofa, watching Food Network for hours, reading trashy romance novels and watching sappy romcoms—all of these things bring me joy. (Yes, I know they reinforce the patriarchy. You win some, you lose some.)

May you ask more and better questions.

Homegirl interventions leave me with more questions than answers. But usually they leave me with far better questions than I began with. May your curiosity be unceasing.

May your rage be a force for good.

What you build is infinitely more important than what you tear down. When the struggle feels unwinnable, may you never forget this one thing:

You got this. We got this.

ACKNOWLEDGMENTS

I learned I would be doing this book on my thirty-fifth birthday. Thanks be to God Herself for awesome birthday gifts like this.

A number of people have cheered me on, listened to me bellyache, and coached me as I have brought this book into the world. Thank you to my agent, the visionary Tanya McKinnon, who called me up and told me that she didn't care what else I had going on. She needed me to focus on and complete this project. For that gentle but firm kick in the pants, I say, Thank you, Tanya. We did it.

My editor, Elisabeth Dyssegaard, is the kind of white girl whom I would absolutely invite to sit on my sofa. Thank you for your care and attention to this project. Thank you to the whole St. Martin's team, especially Martin, Donna, Laura, and Gabi, for bringing this book to fruition.

Clearly, I have the baddest crew of homegirls to ever freaking live. Thank you to my Wonder Twin Susana, my bae Robin, to all my Crunks, to my ratchets Tanisha, Jessica, and Treva, to my Ninjas Joan, Yaba, Kaila, and Esther, to Melanye and Shatema, Leslie, Charisse, and Valerie, Theresa and Candice B, Sheri, Erica, Crystal, and Kristie. Thank you Breana Jeter for helping to inspire these words. Thank you also to Candice F and to Alicia. Some of you read parts of this book, while others of you took the time to cheer me on, commiserate, pray, and make me laugh. It goes without saying that I couldn't have done any of it without all of you.

Thank you to my colleagues at Rutgers and to the School of Arts and Sciences for giving me time off to do a public project.

I have deep gratitude for Michael Eric Dyson and for the generosity and encouragement he offers to a whole generation of young intellectuals that he inspired to dream bigger. He is the first model I had of what it might mean to do work in both the university and the public arenas, and my mind is still blown that today I can call him friend and mentor. This book simply wouldn't have happened without you, Michael.

Thank you also to Melissa Harris-Perry, simply one of the baddest scholars and public intellectuals to ever do it. Thank you for being my friend, big sister, encourager, and mentor, Melissa. You helped inspire the title of this book on a particularly memorable episode of *MHP* where your rage was palpable but delivered with a level of finesse that I have not seen before or since. Thank you for loving us.

Even though everybody still believes that feminists hate men, I have a formidable crew of homeboys and male mentors, too. Thank you to Mychal Denzel Smith, Darnell

Moore, Kiese Laymon, Marlon Peterson, Mark Anthony Neal, and David Ikard. Thank you to Dwayne Betts, Julius Fleming, and Sijuola Crawford for reading this work and sharing your thoughts with me.

Thank you also to my love Raydell. You inspire me to conquer all my fears.

Finally, thank you to the Cooper women. Thank you, Mama, Grandmama, and Aunties, for the model you have so lovingly and unapologetically offered for how to live my absolute best Black-girl life. I love you.